THE LITTLE ROCK ARSENAL CRISIS

THE LITTLE ROCK ARSENAL CRISIS

ON THE PRECIPICE OF THE AMERICAN CIVIL WAR

DAVID SESSER

THE History PRESS

Published by The History Press
Charleston, SC 29403
www.historypress.net

First published 2013

Manufactured in the United States

ISBN 978.1.60949.969.3

Library of Congress CIP data applied for.

Notice: The information in this book is true and complete to the best of our knowledge. It is offered without guarantee on the part of the author or The History Press. The author and The History Press disclaim all liability in connection with the use of this book.

Contents

Acknowledgements

I would like to thank my colleagues at Henderson State University and especially my coworkers at Huie Library, both past and present, for their support with this project. I also need to thank the members of the Henderson Writers Group for their comments and guidance. My parents were instrumental in teaching me about history, and this book would not be possible without them. Finally, my wife, Deborah, encouraged and pushed me to complete this project. Thanks for all of your help.

INTRODUCTION

Arkansas was a young state in 1860. A member of the Union for less than a quarter-century, the state was slow to join its southern companions who were clamoring to leave the United States after the election of Abraham Lincoln. The economy of the state was just getting on solid financial ground, and major gains were seen in the agricultural output between 1850 and 1860. The last vestiges of the frontier were being replaced by an air of respectability. But Arkansas was a divided state. Immense plantations with large slave populations operated across eastern and southern Arkansas while small yeoman farmers hacked out a more meager livelihood in the Ozark and Ouachita mountains. Straddling two distinct geographic areas, settlers in the Arkansas Delta had much more in common with their neighbors in Mississippi and Louisiana than their fellow statesmen to the west.

This divide was based almost exclusively on the two major economic systems that operated in the state. Slavery was the lifeblood of the planters. Without the labor that slaves provided, large-scale farming operations would be prohibitively expensive. Likewise, the use of large numbers of slaves to grow crops in rougher terrain in the western and northern areas of the state would quickly deplete the soil and was also economically unfeasible. As the population of the state grew, this divide only became more apparent. According to the 1840 census, only 40 percent of the total population lived in lowland areas, compared to 60 percent who lived in upland counties. By 1860, this trend had been reversed, with lowland counties now representing

52 percent of the total population in the state while upland counties now only held 48 percent.[1]

Between 1810 and 1860, the population of Arkansas grew from just over 1,000 to more than 435,000. Of these, more than 111,000 were slaves, and 144 residents were classified as free blacks. Extremely rural, the state had only one city with a population over 3,000 in 1860: Little Rock. Clearly, large-scale planting operations were becoming more important in the state's economy as the years passed, and with this economic power came political clout. These changes, coupled with the election of Abraham Lincoln, would eventually lead to the development of the arsenal crisis.[2]

The impact that the Little Rock Arsenal crisis had on the state and its subsequent secession is immeasurable. The first mention of the crisis in post-conflict examination appears in John Harrell's volume on Arkansas during the war. Written as part of a thirteen-volume set, it examined the contributions of each state of the Confederacy and the border states. As a participant in some of the events surrounding the arsenal crisis, Harrell's examination of the events shows that he was not merely an observer. Rather, he noted that he sent a telegraph that might have started the entire chain of events that led to the ultimate seizure of the arsenal. After relating the background and ultimate outcome of the crisis, he concluded by laying the blame for the situation on Abraham Lincoln, whose election was seen by many as the ultimate catalyst for the seizure of the arsenal.[3]

The next work that dealt with the crisis, *Arkansas in War and Reconstruction*, was written by a professor at the University of Arkansas, David Thomas. Published in 1926 and financially supported by the United Daughters of the Confederacy, Thomas's book was the first title written by a scholar that examined the war and Reconstruction in Arkansas. As part of the secession movement, Thomas thought that the actions at the arsenal had little or no impact on the voters of the state supporting a call for a secession convention.[4]

Other examinations of the arsenal crisis appear in Michael Dougan's *Confederate Arkansas*, which examines the arsenal crisis in the overall buildup toward secession. In the first detailed examination of the secession movement in the state, Dougan squarely places the responsibility of the arsenal crisis on the shoulders of Governor Rector. He also agreed with Thomas that the events surrounding the surrender of the post did not push the state toward secession and, in fact, pushed the Unionists in Arkansas to mobilize.[5]

With the exception of works that examine the entire war in the state, another in-depth recounting and analysis of the events at the arsenal has never been published. When a mention does appear, it is often not much more than a few sentences. By closely examining the events that occurred in Little Rock in early 1861, historians can better understand the situation that the citizens of Arkansas found themselves in after the election of Abraham Lincoln.

Chapter 1

Arkansas in Early 1861

It was an election with monumental consequences. With slightly less than 40 percent of the national popular vote, Abraham Lincoln defeated three other candidates to claim the United States presidency. In Arkansas, the state experienced its highest ever voter turnout, but Lincoln did not receive any popular votes from Arkansans, and the state was carried by President James Buchanan's vice president, John C. Breckinridge. But regardless of which candidate carried the state, the Republican from Illinois won a plurality of the national vote as well as more than enough electoral votes and would be sworn into office on March 4, 1861.[6]

Lincoln's election pushed an already divided country even closer to an official separation, and the people of Arkansas wasted little time expressing their opinions on the soon-to-be president and his possible policies. For instance, even before the election was held, some politicians were advocating that, if he should win, Lincoln could be prevented from taking office. Edward W. Gantt, who was elected to represent the state's Second Congressional District in 1860, declared "that he would be in favor of resisting his inauguration by forces of arms." The *Arkansas Gazette* responded by declaring Gantt to be a disunionist and secretly supporting the election of Lincoln to simply gain sympathy to his call for secession. Several newspapers in the state urged their readers to give the new president a chance to lead. Any calls for secession and disunion were answered by numerous calls in support of maintaining the Federal government, at least for the time being. The *Gazette* said, "Lincoln is elected in the manner

Abraham Lincoln's election in November 1860 directly led to the situation in Little Rock.
Photo courtesy of the Library of Congress.

John C. Breckinridge won the popular vote in Arkansas. *Photo courtesy of the Library of Congress.*

prescribed by the law and by the majority prescribed by the Constitution. Let him be inaugurated, let not steps be taken against this administration until he has committed an overt act, which cannot be remedied by law."[7] The state was geographically split, with many secessionists located in the eastern and southern counties where large-scale plantations existed while strong support for the Union held sway in the more mountainous regions in the western and northern areas of Arkansas.[8]

Other newspapers continued to call for calm in the aftermath of Lincoln's election, while the most prominent Arkansan to suggest another course of action was the newly elected governor, Henry M. Rector. In his inaugural address delivered on November 15, 1860, the highest elected official in the state claimed that a split in the country would come sooner or later, and it was better to separate the nation now rather than risk war.[9]

With these statements, Rector openly threw his support behind the steadily growing secessionist movement. The governor needed an issue like secession to solidify his position within the state and in the Democratic Party. Henry Massie Rector was a native Kentuckian who also spent time

Henry Rector. *Photo by David Sesser.*

The Arkansas State Capitol Building, now known as the Old State House. *Photo courtesy of the Library of Congress.*

in Missouri before settling in Arkansas in 1835. Rector's father was a surveyor and land speculator and left large tracts to Henry upon his death. The younger Rector managed this land, farmed and worked as a lawyer before receiving his first political position. In 1842, Rector was named by President John Tyler as the U.S. Marshal for Arkansas. Two terms in the state senate beginning in 1848 followed his service as the marshal, and he also served as a Democratic presidential elector in 1852. In 1854, he moved to Little Rock and represented Pulaski County in the state House of Representatives. Before becoming governor, Rector also served on the state supreme court from 1859 until 1860 but was apparently asked to resign due to incompetence. These claims did not immediately impact Rector's political career, as incompetence mattered less in Arkansas than connections to "the Family."[10]

Political control of Arkansas had rested with "the Family" since before statehood. A group of mostly related and intermarried politicians, the group controlled virtually every level of politics in the state. Aligned with the national Democratic Party, their main opposition within the state was from other factions within the Arkansas Democratic Party and the tiny Whig Party, which was replaced by the American or Know-Nothing Party. Rector was a member of the Family and was related by blood to the first and fifth governors, James and Elias Conway. But by 1860, some politicians in the state saw an opportunity to move away from this dynasty that had controlled Arkansas for so many years. Rector ran as an Independent Democratic candidate for governor against the Family candidate, Richard Johnson. The campaign was confusing for voters as Rector tried to distance himself from his past involvement with the Family and contrast his positions on various issues with the positions he previously held. One of the few newspapers that supported Rector sought to inform its readers about the dark-horse candidate, writing:

> *Who is Henry M. Rector? A poor, honest farmer of Saline County, who toils at the plow handles to provide bread, meat, and raiment for his wife and children. Do you know him? There are many people who do—who have seen him laboring in the fields, earning his bread with sweat of his brow. But possessing the imprint of manhood from nature, and from nature's God, at this country's greatest need, he arose like Cincinnatus of old and did his duty.*

This eloquent and somewhat embellished account tried to tie the gubernatorial candidate with the common yeoman farmers of Arkansas.

These efforts were hurt by other actions, like the confusion Rector had with some of the basic issues. For instance, he initially supported the creation of a system of public education in the state but later changed his mind when he was informed that the plan would increase taxes. Despite these shortcomings, Richard Johnson ultimately ran an even more ineffective campaign, and Rector successfully portrayed himself as a common farmer and not a disgraced former Supreme Court justice, leading to his win on election day. Rector ultimately carried the state with 31,518 votes to Johnson's 28,622. But even as he prepared to take office, Rector realized that while he had control of the governor's office, he did not have a working coalition within the state legislature. The Family still had a sizeable faction within the statehouse, and some legislators would not even speak to the new governor. Without this control and in the face of outright hostility from some legislators, Rector scrambled to identify an issue that he could use to gain support for his vision for the state. The governor ultimately chose the issue of secession to consolidate his power and become an effective chief executive.[11]

Rector was joined in his push for secession by other prominent politicians in the state. Edward Gantt and Thomas C. Hindman, representative for the First Congressional District in the state, spoke before the legislature on November 23 and 24 to push the case for secession. Hindman lived in Helena, which is located in Phillips County on the Mississippi River and served as an important port for the cotton-growing areas in the Delta region of Arkansas. Phillips County was also home to more slaves than any other county in the state in 1860. Gantt resided in Hempstead County, located in the southwestern corner of the state and home to one of the largest slave populations outside of the eastern Delta region. This split between the highland and lowland areas of the state could not be more apparent in the words of these politicians, who both hailed from areas of the state that relied on slavery for much of their economic activity. These two areas of the state stood apart from the upland farming areas and were quite different socially and economically. Secession was much more popular among the planters along the Mississippi, Arkansas, Red and Ouachita Rivers, and support for maintaining the Union was strongest among the small farmers in the more mountainous regions of the state.[12]

The state legislature mostly ignored the governor and the congressmen, continuing with its regular business and spending very little time on any secession-related bills. One topic that the state legislature needed to take

Thomas C. Hindman. Hindman, Thomas C., WICR 31880, in the collection of Wilson's Creek National Battlefield. *Image courtesy of the National Park Service.*

up was the appointment of a new United States senator. Robert Ward Johnson, the older brother of Richard Johnson, the Family candidate who was defeated by Rector for the governorship, was appointed to represent Arkansas in the senate in 1853 and was selected for a full term in 1855. His term ended in 1861, and the state legislature was tasked with selecting his replacement. Rector's lack of influence with the legislature led him to oppose the possibility of a new senator being selected without his input. The governor responded to the situation by returning to the issue of secession and once again asked the legislature to consider leaving the Union.[13]

Continuing to ignore the governor's wishes, five candidates for the senate position addressed the legislature in December, and only one, Rector's choice, openly advocated for secession. The other candidates urged the legislature and citizens of the state to tread carefully and wait to see what impact Lincoln's election would actually have on the citizens of Arkansas. After nine votes, one of the moderate voices, Charles B. Mitchel of Hempstead County, was selected for the position.[14]

At the same time, events across the country began to have an impact on Arkansas's future in the Union. On December 20, 1860, South Carolina became the first state to secede from the Union, and the event was received with enthusiasm by pro-secession factions in Arkansas. Cheered by South Carolina's exit from the Union, citizens in the eastern part of the state began to strongly lobby the legislature for secession or at least to call a secession convention to allow the citizens of Arkansas to decide whether the state should remain as part of the United States. The most effective way to influence both voters and the legislature during this period was through newspaper editorials. Representative Hindman owned the *Old Line Democrat* newspaper in Little Rock, which began to call for secession in every issue. Pro-secession forces were both well organized and well funded, while their pro-Union counterparts were quite disorganized and struggled to get their messages out to the people of Arkansas. Support for the state remaining in the Union continued to appear in the *Arkansas Gazette*, and the editor feared that any attempt at secession would only lead to war, bloodshed and destruction of "commercial and financial interests" of the United States. Petitions supporting the dissolution of the bonds between Arkansas and the Federal government were received from many of the counties in eastern and southern Arkansas that contained large-scale plantations and relied on slave labor to produce cotton and other crops. Even some counties that did not contain large-scale plantations sent petitions to the legislature calling for the opportunity to decide if the state should leave the Union.[15]

After weeks of maneuvering by the governor, petitions from across the state and numerous speakers openly advocating for secession, the legislature decided to allow the citizens of the state to vote on the question of a secession convention. In a bill approved by the state House of Representatives on December 22, 1860, the state senate did not take on the issue until January 16, 1861. When the election was approved, the legislature called for two questions to be put before the voters. The first question was whether a convention should be called. The second question allowed voters to select representatives for the convention, if it were approved. The date of the election was set for February 18, 1861.[16]

Tensions continued to run high as petitions began to pour into the state legislature from Unionist counties in response to the call for an election, and both sides began to mobilize to get the vote out. But while most of the state was preparing for the upcoming election, other events would soon divert the attention of the governor and the legislature and threaten to bring Arkansas into open conflict with the Federal government before any vote could be held to determine the state's future. The United States Arsenal, located in Little Rock, contained thousands of arms and had been completely unmanned until November, when a small detachment of Federal soldiers took control of the post in direct response to the actions of the secessionists in the state. This action, combined with the loud calls for secession from across the state, made Little Rock a tinderbox that threatened to explode in early 1861 and could drag the country into a war where the sides were still unclear.[17]

CHAPTER 2

THE FEDERAL MILITARY POSTS IN ARKANSAS

As the citizens of Arkansas debated whether or not to leave the Union, the Federal government already had a well-established presence in the state. The two most important installations were the United States Arsenal, located in the capital city, and Fort Smith in western Arkansas. Located several blocks from the Arkansas River, the United States Arsenal at Little Rock was an imposing military post tasked with storing weapons and munitions for the United States Army. In 1861, it was an important landmark in the city, and its importance to the defense of both Little Rock and the state as a whole was paramount. Few people realized how important the post would become in the debate over Arkansas's potential secession from the Union and how close the nation came to open warfare over the weapons held in the arsenal.

Located on what was then the frontier, Arkansas shared its western border with the Indian Territory, and a military presence was needed in the state to meet any threats that might exist in that area. The need for such an installation in the capital city was best expressed by the first elected governor of the state, James Sevier Conway, in a letter to the War Department, in which he said, "We trust that the enlightened members of that body [Congress] will not forget the claims of Arkansas upon the public revenue. We are a frontier people exposed to savage invasions and are often in pressing need of assistance and protection which only the Federal government can afford."[18]

With the need for a military post apparent, construction on the arsenal began in 1837, less than one year after Arkansas became the twenty-fifth state to join the Union.[19]

The United States Army sent Major Richard B. Lee to Little Rock to select a site for the arsenal.[20] The major arrived in early 1837 and began to search for suitable sites around the city. Congress appropriated $14,000 for the post, which was to include both the acquisition of the land and the initial buildings on the site. The location that was finally chosen was located south of the city limits of the small village and was being used as a racetrack by the local jockey club. The land was owned by Richard C. Hawkins and was described as "high, beautiful, and commanding, and, in a military, as well as every other point of view, may be considered the most eligible location that could have been made; convenient, while it is sufficiently removed to avoid any contact with the town." This distance between the quickly growing town and the military post was important, as it created a buffer between the local civilians and the soldiers garrisoning the arsenal.[21]

Major Lee purchased the land from Hawkins for $2,400. Little Rock did not lose its racetrack; it was simply moved to a new location. The public in the city supported the idea of establishing an arsenal in the Little Rock area but wanted to ensure that the structure would stand the test of time and adequately meet the needs of the military in the state and nearby Indian Territory. The *Arkansas Gazette* expressed this sentiment, saying, "This frontier must for years to come be the object of peculiar solicitude to the federal government, as well as to the state of Arkansas, and the military works for its protection ought to be durable and respectable, and not a temporary set of huts that soon decay and crumble."[22]

After the initial purchase of the land, little was done on the site for more than a year. Major Lee returned to Washington to discuss the project with the Secretary of War, Joel Roberts Poinsett.[23]

Finally returning to Arkansas in May 1838, the major advertised for bids for building materials to construct the initial structures at the site and set a delivery date of the first materials for November 1. The winning bid was received from William R. Gibson and Stephen Cotter, who charged only $24 per thousand board feet of cypress. The contract was witnessed by William E. Woodruff, publisher of the *Arkansas Gazette*, along with other prominent citizens. With the contract in hand, Major Lee once again departed Arkansas for Washington to obtain additional funding for the completion of the project, as the original $14,000 appropriated for the entire arsenal was found to be insufficient for both the purchase of the land and the construction of the necessary buildings. The first shipment of munitions arrived at the arsenal in June 1838, when one hundred tons was delivered to the post.[24]

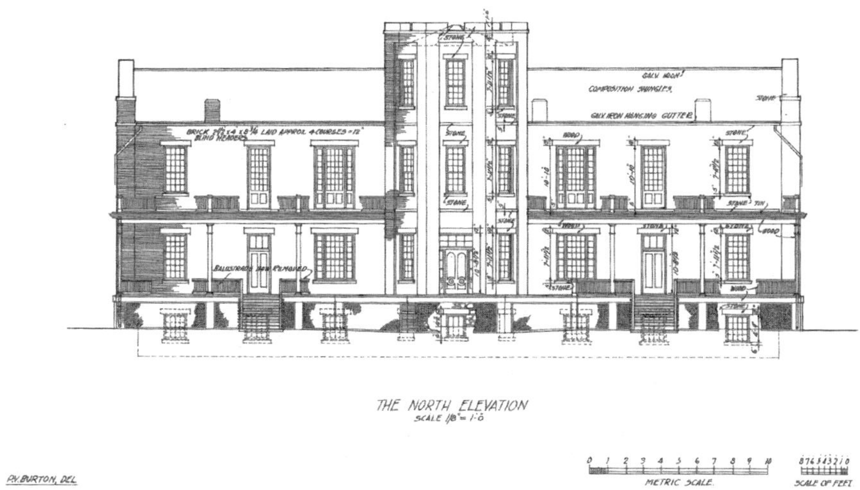

Drawing of the arsenal building. *Courtesy of the Library of Congress.*

The Little Rock Arsenal. *Photo courtesy of the Library of Congress.*

To supervise the construction of the arsenal and act as the master builder, John Warmley Walker was transferred from the arsenal at Baton Rouge, Louisiana. Walker would remain in Arkansas after the completion of his work on the arsenal in Little Rock and would raise his family in the state. The timber used in the construction was from the Pine Bluff area, and it is believed that the bricks were made by Thomas Thornes, who also supplied the bricks for the Old Statehouse in Little Rock.[25]

The main structure of the arsenal became known as the "Tower Building." By 1841, according to the *Arkansas Gazette*, construction on the Tower Building was progressing quickly and would soon be completed. Originally constructed to actually hold the weapons of the arsenal, it was subsequently also used as a barracks for married junior officers. Other buildings were constructed to house more married officers, a barracks for enlisted men and a sutler's store. Assorted outbuildings and stables were completed over time at the complex, for a total of twenty-eight structures by 1860.[26]

While impressive, the Little Rock Arsenal was not the only military post in the state in 1860, or even the most important. Fort Smith had a long and complicated history on the western border of the state. The fort was originally established in 1817 to provide security near the intersection of the Arkansas and Poteau Rivers, and a small settlement soon grew around the military post. The post was named for General Thomas A. Smith, commander of the military district that included the post when it was originally constructed. The fort was abandoned in 1824 as the frontier continued to move westward and the soldiers at the post were needed in the Indian Territory, but the settlers who had moved into the area did not follow the military. Rather, the population lobbied the Federal government to return a military presence to the area. The next group of troops who arrived in the area were garrisoned at the fort in 1831 to ready the post for Choctaws from Mississippi who were being moved to the Indian Territory by the Federal government. The post was abandoned again in 1834 after years of arguments between the officers of the garrison and the whiskey traders in the nearby community. The officers were tasked with

Opposite, top: Part of the original Fort Smith with the Arkansas River in the background. *Photo by David Sesser.*

Opposite, bottom: Initial Point Marker in Fort Smith to identify the boundary between Arkansas and the Indian Territory. *Photo by David Sesser.*

INITIAL POINT

Fort Gibson. *Photo courtesy of the Library of Congress.*

keeping contraband out of the hands of the nearby Indians, as well as their enlisted men, and the frustrations of the job eventually became too much. In response to these problems, a new post was established several miles away in the Indian Territory and was named Fort Coffee. Finally, in 1838, after years of lobbying by settlers in the area, Congress approved the construction of a permanent fort on the western edge of Arkansas, and the location of the old Fort Smith was selected as the site.[27]

The fort was garrisoned from 1838 until 1861. The Federal army stationed multiple units at the fort during this period, and it also acted as a supply point for other garrisons in the Indian Territory. Volunteer units from Arkansas were also no strangers to the post. For more than nine months in 1846–47, five companies of volunteers from across the state manned Fort Smith, as well as Fort Gibson and Fort Wayne in the Indian Territory. The regular soldiers typically stationed at these posts were withdrawn during this period to participate in the Mexican-American War. Over the years, the garrison posted at Fort Smith continued to shrink as the army manned more posts across the frontier. By February 1861, during the secession crisis in Arkansas and other southern states, the garrison at Fort Smith consisted of only two companies of the Second U.S. Cavalry.[28]

Fort Smith. *Photo courtesy of the Library of Congress.*

Fort Smith Barracks. The first floor of this building was constructed in 1851. *Photo by David Sesser.*

Captain James Totten. Totten, James, WICR 31808, in the collection of Wilson's Creek National Battlefield. *Image courtesy of the National Park Service.*

With sectional tensions filling the air, the War Department began to shift some units around to occupy and reinforce particular posts. Fort Smith received additional troops from Fort Leavenworth, Kansas. Some of these troops were eventually transferred again to the Little Rock Arsenal. The men who would occupy the arsenal belonged to Battery F, Second United States Artillery. On November 21, the unit had been ordered to Little Rock. Under the command of Captain James Totten, the unit departed Fort Smith on November 27. Captain Totten had departed on the day that the order was received, in order to spend several days on leave in Little Rock before the arrival of his troops and the commencement of their garrison duty in the city. Command of the unit was passed to First Lieutenant Anderson Merchant and Second Lieutenant St. Clair Searing, who oversaw the transportation of the men and equipment down the Arkansas River. The unit arrived in Little Rock on December 6 and assembled along Markham Street. Met by Captain Totten, he led his men to their new post on the southern edge of the city.

The total number of men stationed at the arsenal in January 1861 was ninety, according to the War Department. This number included both the seventy-six artillerymen directly under Totten's command as part of Battery F as well as members of the ordnance department who were tasked with maintaining the arms stored at the arsenal. Garrisoned through the 1840s, changing priorities in the army led to the withdrawal of troops from the post, and by 1860, the arsenal was manned by just a small staff of caretakers. With the arrival of these new troops, the Little Rock Arsenal held the second-highest number of men of any arsenal, army or depot at this time and was surpassed only by the ninety-three troops stationed at the Augusta, Georgia Arsenal. Several facilities were manned by only a handful of troops, while others were completely empty of soldiers. The transfer of these troops from Fort Leavenworth via Fort Smith shows how important the Federal government thought both the weapons held at the arsenal and Arkansas's loyalty to the Union were. While secessionist voices in the state were loudly calling for the dissolution of the bond between the state and the national government, the fervor in Arkansas did not match the intensity seen in some of the Deep South states during this period. It was believed that not only could these troops protect what belonged to the Federal government, but they might also prove to be a calming influence on the most rabid secessionist citizens in Arkansas and likewise remind others who were still considering the best course of action for the state of both the strength of the army and the importance of the Federal government to the defense of the state.[29]

While the army typically did not have many troops stationed at the arsenal, it was nevertheless well stocked with a variety of weapons and munitions at this time. The last available complete inventory of the weapons held by the arsenal dates to November 12, 1859, and lists several hundred weapons on hand. In the report, the arsenal reported holding 349 muskets of .69 caliber and 54 rifles of .54 caliber. On December 30, 1859, the War Department ordered the Springfield and Watertown Armories in Massachusetts and the Watervliet Armory in New York to distribute 115,000 arms to arsenals located throughout the South. This action was undertaken shortly after John Brown's failed raid on the United States Arsenal located at Harper's Ferry, Virginia. The United States Arsenal in Little Rock did not receive

Waterv liet Arsenal, New York. *Photo courtesy of the Library of Congress.*

Augusta Arsenal. *Photo courtesy of the Library of Congress.*

any additional arms from this shipment, but other reports show that the number of weapons at the post would continue to grow over the next several years. On January 21, 1861, a new report was delivered to the House of Representatives of the United States Congress that detailed the number of arms held by the Federal government across the country. A total of 1,364 percussion small arms were held in Arkansas at this time. Of these weapons, 54 were rifles, which also appeared on the 1859 report for the Little Rock Arsenal. An additional 1,310 muskets appear on the inventory. It is unclear if these weapons were held at the arsenal in Little Rock or if this number included both the weapons at that location as well as at Fort Smith. These totals did not include any flintlock arms or revolvers, which were held at both installations. Also appearing on the inventory at this time were ten pieces of brass field artillery. Six of these weapons were located at Fort Smith and likely belonged to Battery E of the Second U.S. Artillery, the sister unit of Battery F in Little Rock. Four guns were also located at the arsenal for use by Totten's men.[30]

The number of weapons held in Arkansas did not approach the total that other southern states possessed but was a sizeable prize for any force that might capture them. In contrast, North Carolina held more than 36,000 small arms and a total of 41 pieces of artillery within her borders. Virginia possessed only 17,000 small arms, but more than 860 cannons were in the state in 1861. The weapons at the Little Rock Arsenal and other Federal posts throughout the South were an important part of the United States Army's fighting ability, and the capture of those weapons by states as they departed the Union would leave the national government in a precarious position if hostilities did break out. It is also important to note that the weapons stored across the nation did not belong to the individual states where they were housed but rather to the Federal government. According to the Militia Act of 1812, each state in the Union was authorized a dollar amount for weapons to protect itself. These weapons were drawn from national arsenals based on their monetary value and transferred to each individual state. However, control of the weapons remained with the Federal government. They were stored in a state arsenal and were available for the state militia to use in the case of an emergency. Small militia armories also existed across the country for the storage of weapons owned by individual units, and these weapons and training were the responsibility of those units. Authorized by the state, these units purchased their weapons and were also tasked with maintaining meeting places to conduct drill and hold other functions. The weapons owned by militia units were typically—but not always—older and less reliable than those owned by the War Department. With such a prize available for the taking, it seemed only prudent that a force would arrive in the city to ensure the safety of the weapons.[31]

While the weapons held by the arsenal in Little Rock were typically unguarded with only a caretaker staff on the premises, the threat of secession pushed the Federal army to supplement the installation with troops from Kansas via Fort Smith. The artillerymen tasked with manning the arsenal were regular, professional soldiers. Their commander, Captain James Totten, was not unfamiliar to the citizens of Little Rock. His father was a local physician and also served at the arsenal earlier during his career. His son's leave of absence from his unit in November was spent with his parents at their home in the city. Totten was born in Pittsburgh, Pennsylvania, on September 11, 1818. Little is known about his early life, but Totten was admitted to the United States Military Academy at West Point, graduating in 1841. Commissioned as a second lieutenant, he was promoted to first lieutenant in 1847. Between 1849 and 1850, Totten served in Florida and help suppress uprising by the Seminole Indians. Totten received another promotion in 1855, this time to the rank of captain. He was stationed from 1857 to 1858 in Kansas, where he and his battery were involved in the "Bloody Kansas" conflict. Earlier in 1860, Totten helped expel non-Indians from reservation land in Kansas. When he arrived in Little Rock, Totten was no stranger to defending the interests of the Federal government from actions taken by private citizens from his recent experiences in Kansas, and the actions that would follow his posting in Arkansas would prove to be no different.[32]

With his arrival in Little Rock, Totten and his men quickly and quietly manned the arsenal and settled into a normal garrison routine with limited interaction with the residents of the city. The arsenal was still near the outskirts of the city, and the need to interact with the local population was minimal. However, over the years since the site had originally been selected and the arsenal was constructed, Little Rock had continued to grow, and now the post was surrounded by private homes on both the north and west sides. About three blocks away to the east of the arsenal grounds stood St. John's College, the first institution of higher learning in the city. Any attack on the post and subsequent defense would likely lead to civilian casualties. As the majority of the soldiers posted at the arsenal were artillerymen, they were most familiar with those weapons. However, the use of cannons in a city setting was out of the question in the mind of Totten. He continued to prepare for the worst and made defensive preparations to the best of his ability.[33]

The placement of troops in Little Rock was ordered in direct response to the rumblings of secession that were emanating from Arkansas and the other southern states and to protect the arms held in the city. The War Department made a decision to actively protect the weapons and munitions stored across the South as a show of strength to the local populations. Little did they realize that this action would have potentially explosive consequences in Arkansas. A growing distrust of the Federal government, especially the Lincoln administration scheduled to take office in March, made the posting of troops to the arsenal a potential nightmare for Totten and his superiors. This was also coupled with a governor with little influence but with the desire to make his mark on the state amid growing calls for secession.

Some citizens of Arkansas began to view the posting of troops at the arsenal as an attack on the sovereignty of their state and decided to respond in kind. The first moves were made to send militia and volunteer units to the capital to capture the weapons held in the arsenal and to capture or force the Federals tasked with protecting its contents to flee the state. After remaining relatively unnoticed for more than three months, once the pro-secessionist population in the state did begin to pay attention to the arsenal, the presence of the Federal troops in the city quickly made an already unstable situation even more likely to bring about bloodshed.

Chapter 3

Volunteer Militia Units Arrive in Little Rock

The arrival of Federal forces in Little Rock in December 1860 set into motion events that would threaten to lead to open conflict in the streets of Arkansas's capital city. Other events across the country would divert national attention away from the precarious and volatile conditions in Arkansas, but the citizens of the state found themselves caught up in the struggle to claim possession of the Little Rock Arsenal with the population of the capital city stuck in the middle between two opposing forces. The Federal troops faced off against volunteer militia units from communities across the state, and the prospect of more troops arriving to reinforce their Arkansas brethren would eventually force Captain James Totten of the Federal army to consider other solutions to defending the arsenal with force.

While the Federal soldiers had been stationed at the arsenal for almost two months, the interaction between the military men and the local population had been limited. The arrival of native son Totten in Little Rock had been greeted with happiness, and the event was celebrated at numerous social gatherings that lasted the entire month and were part of Christmas festivities. Totten's father's standing in the community had a positive impact on the situation, but this was not destined to last.[34]

The first correspondence between Captain Totten and the government of Arkansas was exchanged on January 28, 1861. Governor Henry Rector recognized that the presence of the Federal troops now stationed at the arsenal could prove to be advantageous to his goal of gathering popular and political support for the cause of Arkansas secession. While Rector did not have any evidence that the people of Arkansas wished to leave the Union, as the popular referendum to select representatives on the subject had not yet been held, this did not deter him from warning Totten about the disposition of the weapons at the arsenal. Writing to Totten, Rector claimed the "U.S. Arsenal at this place will be permitted to remain in the possession of the Federal officers until the State, by authority of the people, shall have determined to sever their connection with the General Government." With this opening statement, the governor made the outcome of Arkansas's secession seem to be much more likely than it actually was. Rector continued, saying that the situation would remain stable as long as the troops under Totten's command did not try to move or destroy the weapons and other items held in the arsenal and the current garrison was not reinforced by additional Federal troops. The governor closed by calling for Totten to publically agree to these conditions and "quiet the public mind and prevent a collision between the sovereign people of Arkansas and the Government troops now stationed at this point."[35]

Totten received the letter and almost immediately forwarded the governor's correspondence to Colonel Samuel Cooper, adjutant general of the United States Army in Washington. He included in the message his reply to Rector, writing the next day that he could not "give your Excellency any assurances as to what instructions may in the future be issued regarding this arsenal and the Federal troops now stationed here." Totten continued by reminding the governor "that as an officer in the Army of the United States, that my allegiance is to that Government in whose [service] I am, and that I act by its authority and permission," reinforcing the point that he answered to the Federal government and not the state of Arkansas. The officer closed his communication with the governor by agreeing that he too wished to prevent any possible violence and would do everything in his power to avoid such an occurrence. These letters between Captain Totten and Governor Rector were the start of a correspondence that would last more than a week and chronicled the deteriorating situation in Little Rock.[36]

Rector's initial demands to Totten were unreasonable and could not be met by the captain. The governor all but claimed the weapons for the state but agreed to allow the Federal soldiers at the arsenal to remain in charge of the munitions until the people of Arkansas decided to leave the Union. This claim by Rector was a bit premature, as the first secession convention in the state would later prove. Rector continued with his claims of ownership of the weapons by suggesting that any reinforcement of the garrison at the arsenal or the destruction of any of the materials held at the post would bring about a change in circumstances. These actions were in violation of the Militia Act of 1812, which made clear that the weapons in the arsenal belonged to the Federal government and not the state in which the weapons were located.

Totten responded to the governor's note and reminded the chief executive that the materials at the arsenal belonged to the Federal government and that his loyalties as an officer in the United States Army remained with that institution. He also attempted to placate Rector by claiming that he did not have any information about either the arrival of additional troops or the ordered destruction of any of the weapons. The captain closed his communication by agreeing with the governor on one major point: the mission of both men was to prevent the spilling of blood over the disposition of the Little Rock Arsenal. Totten was not known for his civil tongue, but this situation called for it. Later, during his service in Missouri during the Civil War, Totten became popular for the way he incorporated curse words into his commands, and it was alleged that many soldiers would travel from their units just to hear the officer issue orders to his men for five minutes.[37]

With the initial exchange of correspondence complete, Totten waited for instructions from his commander in Washington. Communication between Little Rock and points to the east was improving during this period. In late 1860, a telegraph wire was extended from Memphis to the town of Des Arc, located northeast of the capital on the White River. Work continued through the winter to bring the service all the way to the city, but with the line only fifty miles away, news about the quickly unfolding events on the Eastern seaboard reached Arkansans faster than ever. This telegraph line allowed communications from the residents of the state to also quickly reach recipients located in other states, a fact that undoubtedly cheered Totten as he struggled to keep possession of the arsenal and desperately waited for instructions. The line finally reached Little Rock on January 30, one day after the first exchange of letters between Totten and Rector, ensuring that any developments within the state could quickly reach Totten's superiors and the rest of the Federal government in Washington.[38]

In his letter of January 29 to Colonel Cooper, Totten practically begged for instructions and enclosed the letters exchanged between the governor and himself, writing, "Most positive and unequivocal instructions are called for, in order that I may not mistake the intentions of the administration regarding the matter at issue." Stationed in a city where his command was potentially surrounded by enemy combatants in a yet-undeclared war,

Memphis before the war, *Harper's Weekly*, March 15, 1862. *Photo courtesy of the Library of Congress.*

168

HARPER'S WEEKLY.

[March 15, 1862.

...ayon.—[See Page 162.]

Totten was extremely cautious and wisely passed any potential decisions up his chain of command.[39]

Totten mentioned in his communication with Cooper that he wished to not mistake the intentions of the current administration, as he knew that Lincoln would not take office until March. The sitting chief executive, President James Buchanan, was in his last weeks in office. Once known as the most qualified man to ever serve as president, Buchanan was a former state legislator, United States representative and senator, secretary of state and minister to both Russia and the Court of St. James. He was selected by the Democratic Party as its candidate in 1856 after it failed to re-nominate the sitting president, Franklin Pierce. Buchanan defeated John C. Fremont, former senator from California and the first ever nominee of the Republican Party, and former president Millard Fillmore, who was the nominee of the Know-Nothing Party. The election was closer than many expected due to the increasing regional tensions that existed in the country. Fremont's campaign was based on stopping the expansion of slavery and supported the repeal of the Kansas-Nebraska Act. This legislation allowed the voters in these territories to decide by popular sovereignty if slavery would be allowed within their borders. This would completely undo the work completed in 1820 that brought about the Missouri Compromise, which banned slavery in the land of the Louisiana Purchase north of 36°30′. The passage of the act created an even deeper split in the country and the Democratic Party in particular. Buchanan was untouched by this controversy, however, as he was serving as the representative of the United States government in England at the time. Buchanan won the election with 45 percent of the popular vote and 174 electoral votes. Fremont received the second highest number of votes, with 33 percent of the popular vote and 114 electoral votes. Fillmore won almost 900,000 popular votes but did not receive any electoral votes. The combined totals of the popular vote won by the other two candidates easily overshadowed Buchanan's winning total.[40]

The new president faced problems from almost his first day in office. The Dred Scott decision was handed down by the United States Supreme Court on March 6, 1857, two days after Buchanan was inaugurated, and the landmark decision declared that Congress could not exclude slavery from any territories. The president then became entangled in the struggle in Kansas Territory over the question of slavery. With the voters of the territory now responsible for determining if slavery would be allowed within its borders, violence broke out between abolitionist and proslavery forces. Buchanan endorsed a proslavery constitution for the state, which had been fraudulently passed and was

President James Buchanan. *Photo courtesy of the Library of Congress.*

eventually not accepted by the House of Representatives. These actions on the issue of slavery by the president further split the Democratic Party. A financial panic in 1857 and other events during the first two years of Buchanan's term allowed Republicans to win control of the House in the election of 1858. With this power, the Republicans tried to block much of Buchanan's legislation. After the election of 1860, Buchanan was unable to stop the country from splitting apart. After the election of Abraham Lincoln, the United States Army lost almost all of its facilities located in the South, but these installations were actually captured or abandoned during the closing days of the Buchanan administration. A lack of leadership from the administration in office was at least partly to blame during the Little Rock Arsenal crisis.[41]

With the situation continuing to deteriorate across the country, Totten waited to hear back from Washington as events continued to unfold in Arkansas. The arrival of the telegraph line in Little Rock was received with great joy by the citizens of the city. To mark the occasion of the first communication sent from the state's capital, John M. Harrell, the local United States attorney, was asked to compose the message. A native of North Carolina, Harrell was a product of the University of Nashville and had lived in Arkansas since 1853. After much deliberation, Harrell decided that he should stick to the news of the day and share the current events of Arkansas with the wider world. When he arrived at the telegraph office, Harrell already had his message composed. He reported that Charles Mitchel had been selected by the state legislature to succeed Robert Johnson in the United States Senate, and then he moved to the events surrounding the arrival of Federal troops at the arsenal the previous month. Harrell claimed that more troops were currently en route from Fort Gibson in the Indian Territory to reinforce the installation. Furthermore, he claimed that all of the western outposts of the army were being abandoned and the troops that were stationed on the frontier to protect settlers from Indian attacks were now on their way to Fort Smith. Another rumor that the attorney shared over the telegraph was that the entire garrison of Fort Smith had been transferred to Little Rock to man the arsenal. Harrell closed his communication with a few bits of true information, including the fact that he had resigned from his post as U.S. attorney upon the election of Abraham Lincoln. Harrell would become the solicitor-general for the State of Arkansas and would later serve in the Confederate army as a colonel.[42]

It is unknown where Harrell received his information about the possible arrival of troops from Fort Gibson or other posts. It is likely that he simply repeated rumors that were traveling through the city and reported them as fact in his telegram. Only a few bits of the information he shared were actually true. But with the entire state on edge about the election of Lincoln and the upcoming secession convention, any rumors about the approach of additional troops were not to be taken lightly.

While the telegraph line that now reached Little Rock originated in Memphis, other cities in the state also had access to the new communication technology. One of the settlements already connected to Memphis was Helena, home of Congressman Thomas C. Hindman and a hotbed of secessionist fervor. In honor of the completion of the line between Little Rock and Memphis, the telegraph office in the Tennessee city opened its lines and allowed every city in Arkansas to listen in on what the capital city had to say. The information that more troops were currently on the way to reinforce the arsenal was not received in a positive manner in Helena.[43]

A mass meeting was immediately held in the Mississippi River town, and the gathered citizens returned to their local telegraph office with a message for Governor Rector. They offered the services of five hundred troops from their city to move on the arsenal and forcibly take the installation from the Federal forces under Totten in order to seize the weapons for the state. While addressed to the governor, the communication was first delivered to Edmund Burgevin, Rector's brother-in-law and the adjutant general of the Arkansas Militia. Any request made by the governor for troops would be dispatched through Burgevin, and likewise, an offer of military support from the citizens of the state was routed through the military commander.[44]

Burgevin immediately took the communication to Rector, who pondered what response he should dispatch to Helena and any other location that might make a similar offer. The governor was in a precarious position. His communications with Totten so far during the crisis had not produced any positive results. The army officer was steadfast in his refusal to surrender the arsenal or act in any manner that would turn the weapons over to Rector. Arkansas was a member of the Union, and while the state legislature had called for the citizens to approve or dismiss the calls for a secession convention, that vote had not yet taken place. By this point, South Carolina was not the only state to depart from the Union. Mississippi, Florida, Alabama, Georgia and Louisiana had all seceded by January 30, 1861. These states differed from Arkansas, as they were all part of the Deep South rather than the upland South. While Arkansas certainly had areas within its borders that were indistinguishable from areas in Mississippi and Louisiana, not all of the state depended on the type of large-scale plantation operations that existed in the Delta region. Small, yeoman farmers in the Ozark and

Ouachita Mountains did not share many of the same economic and social interests of the planters in Helena and other Mississippi River towns. Other Upland Southern states such as Virginia, Missouri, and Tennessee were also still debating whether or not to leave the Union. If Rector accepted troops to help take the arsenal and Arkansas remained in the Union, the action could be seen as an act of rebellion. However, if the troops assembled in Little Rock on their own accord and not at the behest of the governor, then Rector felt he would be in the clear, regardless of the outcome.

With this in mind, Rector authorized a reply to be sent to the citizens in Helena. The governor told Burgevin to "frame a dispatch as follows: 'The governor has no authority to summon you to take possession of a Federal post, whether threatened to be reinforced or not. Should the people assemble in their own defense, the governor will interpose his official position in their behalf.'"[45]

The reply was purposely vague and allowed Rector to claim to be no part of the arrival of any armed parties in Little Rock. The people of Helena, however, did not find the reply to be vague and instead took the communication as an implicit endorsement of their wishes to move on the capital. The white men of the city began to assemble their weapons and prepared to move out at once. Two militia units were dispatched from Helena. One was called the Philips County Guards, after the local government area Helena served as the seat. The second unit was called the Yell Rifles. This company was named for Archibald Yell, the second governor of Arkansas and former congressman who was killed at the Battle of Buena Vista during the Mexican-American War.[46]

The Yell Rifles were commanded by a thirty-two-year-old Irishman who would go on to become one of the best-known Confederate commanders during the Civil War. Patrick Ronayne Cleburne was born in County Cork, Ireland, in 1828, the son of a Protestant doctor. Cleburne was expected to follow in his father's footsteps and served as an apprentice to a physician for two years but failed the entrance exam for Apothecary Hall, Trinity College, in Dublin. Filled with shame, he enlisted in the British Forty-first Regiment of Foot rather than return home. Reaching the rank of corporal, Cleburne served for more than three years on garrison duty in Ireland during the Great Famine and returned home to find his family on the edge of financial ruin. Cleburne and three of his siblings immigrated to the United States, arriving in New Orleans on Christmas Day in 1849. Traveling up the Mississippi, Cleburne was able to put his medical training to use and obtained a position at a drugstore. He became an American citizen in 1855

Patrick Cleburne. *Photo courtesy of the Library of Congress.*

and joined the Arkansas bar the next year. He and future congressman Thomas C. Hindman partnered in a law practice, and Cleburne was even wounded in an attack by a political opponent of Hindman's on a Helena street. Cleburne killed his attacker and was later cleared by a grand jury of any charges. The two men became even more well known in 1855, when a yellow fever epidemic broke out in the town and both volunteered to stay behind to care for the sick as Helena was evacuated. Cleburne and Hindman were both Democrats, although Cleburne was vocally opposed to slavery. Hindman was a slave owner and supported the institution, but this difference of opinions did not have a negative impact on the men's relationship. As an Irishman, the struggle between the citizens of Cleburne's home country and the British Empire had a deep impact on him. Cleburne believed that local communities should have the rights and responsibilities to live in the manner in which they chose, leading him to accept slavery in the South as a way of life for the time being. During the Civil War, Cleburne would become one of the few Confederate commanders to call for the emancipation and arming of slave men in order for the Confederacy to win the war.[47]

Due to his military service in the British army, Cleburne was elected as captain of the Yell Rifles, a militia unit formed in Helena in the spring of 1860. As the commanding officer, he was responsible for ensuring that his unit was well drilled and ready to respond to any possible emergency. Cleburne and his men decided that the presence of Federal troops at the United States Arsenal in Little Rock and the reply by the governor to their inquiry seemed to support the idea that their services were needed in Little Rock. With the possibility of secession on the horizon for the state, the drill schedule for the Yell Rifles increased, and the 115 men of the unit continued to clamor for the opportunity to throw the Federals out of the arsenal.[48]

As a volunteer unit, the Yell Rifles were responsible for procuring their own supplies, and with the exact situation in Little Rock unknown, the men spread across Helena to gather their martial materials. To prepare for the journey to Little Rock, Cleburne bought a horse, a comforter, a box of wads, two pounds of shot for his pistol, a box of percussion caps and a set of buttons for his uniform. The Helena units formed up and marched down to the Mississippi River, where they boarded the steamboat *Fredrick Notrobe*, which took them downstream to Napoleon, Arkansas. The boat then steamed up the Arkansas River and arrived in Little Rock late on the night of Monday, February 5, 1861. The citizens of the city woke the next morning to find hundreds of armed men milling about in the street.[49]

The two companies of militia from Helena were not the only forces that had descended on the city. Other units began to stream into the capital, mostly from areas that both were heavily in favor of secession and relied on large populations of slaves to produce crops. These men were there in response not only to Rector's claim that he could not prevent them from assembling for their own defense but also because of an incident that occurred during the first three days of February.

While Governor Rector claimed that he did not invite the militia units to the city, his actions before the first groups arrived in Little Rock demonstrated that he was serious when he stated that he did not desire the presence of any additional Federal troops at the arsenal. A rumor spread through the capital on February 2 and 3 that a steamer called the *S.H. Tucker* was making its way up the Arkansas River and carried a unit that was destined to reinforce Captain Totten. A local citizen reported to the governor that he learned that the boat, named for a Little Rock merchant, had passed Pine Bluff and was continuing to ascend the river with between three and four hundred troops on board. Rector asked the informant to put his statement in writing so it would be preserved in case any subsequent actions based on the information led to war and filed it away. The threat of armed conflict breaking out was now more likely than at any point previously in the crisis. Still, the state's chief executive felt that the approach of more troops "seemed improbable," especially from the east, not the forts to the west of Little Rock. Nevertheless, Rector ordered three cannons manned by local volunteers to be wheeled to the riverbank near a wharf close to downtown Little Rock in anticipation of the arrival of the steamboat. He also ordered messengers to be sent to find the boat, if it existed. By February 3, it became apparent that the rumor was unfounded, and the cannons were fired in order to unload them and were removed from their location along the river. As the rumored Federal troops did not arrive in the city, bloodshed was averted for the time being. The *Arkansas State Gazette* later related the events, writing, "It appears that a rumor had gained credence that the *S.H. Tucker* was on her way to this city with a large body of U.S. soldiers, for the purpose of reinforcing the Arsenal at this place…every arrangement was made to effectually resist her approach—and the *Tucker* didn't come."

However, the rumor of reinforcements continued to spread across the state, and even more militia troops continued to appear in the city.[50]

In addition to the troops from militia units from Helena, other men from Jefferson, Prairie, White, Monroe, Hot Spring, Saline, Montgomery and St. Francis Counties had also moved to the capital city. While secessionist sentiments were strongest in the eastern and southern parts of the state, the militia units that arrived in Little Rock were more geographically diverse and included men from upland counties. Montgomery County for instance, located in mountainous western Arkansas, did not have any large-scale plantations, and in 1860, less than two thousand people lived within its borders. But while the question of secession had not yet been decided in the state, many of the citizens of Arkansas felt that any interference from the Federal government in local affairs should be avoided until the voters went to the polls on February 18. By seizing the arsenal and taking its arms for the defense of the state, the people could assert their independence from the Federal government. While secession was an important issue that the voters would tackle in a few weeks, until that time, most of Arkansas was united in the opinion that they should be able to determine their future without any Federal intervention.[51]

As troops continued to arrive in the city, the correspondence between Rector and Totten continued, and the army officer also kept his superiors apprised of the situation. The citizens of Little Rock were becoming more uncomfortable as the days passed and the tension mounted. The actions and words of the governor centered on the arsenal, but any act of violence at the post threatened the safety of the entire city. On February 5, the city council addressed the situation for the first time. Rector later informed Totten of the actions of the Little Rock City Council, which passed a resolution asking that the governor step into the fray and organize a peaceful compromise between the militia units and the Federal soldiers. Rector sent Totten a copy of the resolution, which read that the governor should organize an attempt to take the arsenal by force if "impending danger or necessity" required it. But the council added that any unauthorized attempt to take the arsenal would be viewed as a move to damage the case for state rights and would instead be seen as an insult to the governor. With the city fathers understandably worried about the potential for bloodshed in the streets, Rector called for Totten to follow the advice of the city council and surrender the arsenal to avoid any bloodshed.[52]

The next day, the council passed a much more extensive preamble and resolution that addressed the situation in greater detail, reading in part that the militia units were in the city "under the apprehension that the arsenal and the arms and the munitions of war stored therein may at no distant day be used to the injury of the people of this State." The resolution called for an end to the possibility of hostilities as it "would involve the destruction of much of the property of private citizens of Little Rock, and the loss of many lives of our citizens," as well as the lives of the Federal soldiers. By the day the second resolution was written and approved by the city council, Governor Rector claimed at least some responsibility for the volunteer troops in the city with the support of the council. With the chief executive now taking charge of this suddenly found authority, the council closed by calling on Rector to continue to work with Totten to avoid "a collision and the deplorable consequences that would inevitably result from it."[53]

While the first resolution passed on February 5 by the council called on both parties to work together to prevent an armed conflict from erupting in the city, a second resolution was also passed by the council on the same day. Written during a mass meeting on the subject, the resolution called on Governor Rector to clarify his role in the current situation and either take command of the militia units in the city or order them to withdraw. Rector still claimed that he did not invite the militia units to the city, but the council replied "that it is the duty of the governor to assume the responsibility of this movement or to interpose his authority and influence to prevent it."

The resolution continued by imploring Rector to make an official demand of surrender to Totten. At this point in the crisis, Rector had only called for Totten to not destroy or move the weapons and for the troops already at the arsenal to not be reinforced. On the same day that the second resolution was passed by the council, Rector sent a demand for surrender to Totten.[54]

While the citizens and elected officials of Little Rock wished to prevent any possible bloodshed in their streets, the resolutions that were passed by the city council gave their blessing to Rector to end the situation as quickly as possible but only if such an ending was in favor of the militia units.

The situation was becoming more tenuous for Captain Totten and his soldiers by the minute. Every piece of correspondence that he received from Rector or other parties was forwarded to Washington, but apparently the line of communication ran in only one direction. More than a week had passed from the first exchange between Totten and Rector, and the captain still waited to receive a reply from his superiors. Without these instructions, the soldiers were powerless to act and could only guess at the intentions of the adjutant general.

To the men manning the arsenal, it seemed that the entire state was organizing to seize the post by force. Not only were the number of militia units ever increasing, but also the citizens of Little Rock through their elected officials made it clear that they expected the governor to secure the arsenal for the state. Without any hope of reinforcements, the men at the arsenal could not hold their position against the overwhelming odds they faced. Totten knew he had to find a peaceful solution to the standoff.

Chapter 4

The Arsenal Surrenders and War Is Avoided

By February 5, 1861, Captain James Totten was in an extremely precarious position. Ordered to garrison the United States Arsenal at Little Rock, he and his men had not received any orders in days and the situation around the post continued to deteriorate as more militia units from around the state arrived in the city. The lack of communication from his superiors worried Totten, as he knew that if he followed his orders to the letter and defended the post from an expected assault from the massing volunteers, the long-dreaded war would see its first shots fired in Arkansas. The captain and his men desperately wanted to avoid such a situation and continued to telegraph Washington for further instructions. As the tensions continued to rise between the Federal soldiers and the pro-secessionist units, on February 6, the Little Rock City Council called out its own militia unit, the Capitol Guards, to help keep the peace.

The Capitol Guards were originally formed in Little Rock in 1836, the same year Arkansas joined the Union. The unit's first captain soon resigned, and command passed to a local attorney named Albert Pike. Officially named the First Company of Arkansas Artillery, the unit was soon also known as "Pike's Artillery" in honor of its commander. Originally organized to replace Federal troops on the frontier who were dispatched to Florida to participate in the Seminole War, the unit was actually only called on to lend a martial air to local festivities and hosted a number of well-attended balls.[55]

With the outbreak of war with Mexico in 1846, the Capitol Guards saw their first active service. The Federal government called on Arkansas to

Albert Pike. *Photo courtesy of the Library of Congress.*

furnish a regiment of cavalry and a battalion of infantry to supplement the regular army. The cavalry unit would muster at Washington in southwestern Arkansas and prepare to join units from other states marching to the border. The infantry unit was tasked with replacing regular Federal troops at Fort Smith, who would then be free to join the army being formed in Texas. Captain Pike wanted his unit to serve in the infantry battalion in order to remain close to his growing law practice in Little Rock. The rest of the unit, now known as the Little Rock Guards, had other ideas, however. Not content to guard Fort Smith, the members of the company requested to be accepted as a unit of "flying artillery," and if this was not possible, they wished to enlist together as a company of cavalry. Governor Thomas Drew allowed the unit to join the Arkansas cavalry regiment, and after mustering at the Little Rock Arsenal, the Little Rock Guards departed the capital city on June 20, 1846.[56]

The Arkansas Volunteer Cavalry Regiment departed Washington on July 18 and marched to San Antonio, Texas, to join the Federal army massing for an invasion of Mexico. Former Arkansas governor Archibald Yell was elected as colonel of the regiment, but the lack of military experience among the field officers of the unit was soon apparent. A regular officer wrote that the Arkansans were "wholly without instruction and Colonel Yell is determined to keep them in that condition." Pike sought field rank within the regiment, but as a Whig in an overwhelmingly Democratic unit, his chances of obtaining the colonelcy or any other position were slim. Pike would have been a good choice for a higher command within the Arkansas Regiment. His unit was the most professional group in the regiment, and the Little Rock Guards were the only unit to continue to drill on a regular basis while their comrades took shelter from the intense Texas heat under shade trees.[57]

Part of an army under the command of General John Wool, the Arkansans began to march southward into Mexico to support the advance of General Zachary Taylor's army that continued to fight eastward from the Gulf of Mexico across the country to capture Mexico City. For several months, the Americans advanced into Mexico without finding many signs of the enemy, and the only action any of the Arkansans saw during the first days in Mexico was the capture of Major Solon Borland of the regiment and thirty-four of his men while they slept.[58]

Finally facing the Mexican Army at the Battle of Buena Vista, the Little Rock Guards were separated from the Arkansas regiment before the engagement and attached to the Second United States Dragoons. During the battle, the remainder of the Arkansas regiment retreated in confusion

Top left: General John Wool. *Photo courtesy of the Library of Congress.*

Top right: Solon Borland. *Photo courtesy of the Library of Congress.*

Left: John Selden Roane. *Photo courtesy of the Library of Congress.*

in the face of a Mexican attack, and Colonel Yell was killed while trying to rally his men. The Little Rock Guards, joined by the Second Dragoons and the First Mississippi Rifles, under the command of Colonel Jefferson Davis, repelled the attack and saved the day for the Americans.[59]

Soon after the battle ended, Pike wrote a letter that was published in the *Arkansas Gazette* laying the blame for the Arkansans' retreat squarely on the shoulders of the field officers. With Colonel Yell killed in the battle and Major Borland captured before the army arrived at Buena Vista, the blame fell on Lieutenant Colonel John Selden Roane. Other soldiers in the regiment responded that the Little Rock Guards did not take any active role in the engagement and could not claim any honor in the successful outcome. Eventually, a court of inquiry was convened, and Pike defended his statements about the conduct of the company and Roane accepted the explanation. Regardless of the outcome of the court, the division that existed between the Little Rock Guards and the rest of the Arkansans in the regiment only deepened.[60]

With the conclusion of the court of inquiry, the Little Rock Guards and most of the rest of the Arkansas Regiment ended their active service and returned to Little Rock with the body of Colonel Yell. Rumors continued to fly however, and eventually led to a duel between Pike and Roane near Fort Smith about three weeks after their return to the state. Neither man was able to wound his opponent, and the matter was finally dropped. Pike eventually ended his association with the Little Rock Guards, but his impact on the organization would continue to be felt for years to come.[61]

The unit underwent another name change sometime in the 1850s and became known as the Capitol Guards, as it was called at the time of the arsenal crisis. Continuing to serve as an active militia unit, the Guards also returned to their place in Little Rock society after returning from the war and frequently attended social events as a group around the city. The roster consisted of young men from the best and most influential families from across Little Rock. The unit continued to drill on a regular basis and was considered one of the most professional militia units in the state immediately before the war. It was with this professionalism in mind that the city fathers decided to use the unit near the arsenal. Activated by the city council, the unit assembled on the lawn of their captain, Gordon Peay. After informing his men of the situation and relating the wishes of the council, the unit took up positions between the arsenal and the other militia units that continued to flood into the city.[62]

Few if any of the Capitol Guards called out in 1861 had served in the unit during the Mexican War. However, the men still considered themselves to be more professional than the armed civilians arriving in the capital city from around the state. Many of the militia members from across the state likewise had not served in the previous conflict, but the bitter blood among the Little Rock unit and the other groups continued to run deep. The divide that existed between the citizens of Little Rock and other settlers across the state was more apparent when viewed in the context of the Capitol Guards and the units from Helena and other locations in Arkansas. Little Rock, while still somewhat a rough frontier city, was the pinnacle of civilized society in the state.

The 1860 census showed only 3,700 white residents and 1,100 slaves residing in the city, which was clustered near the Arkansas River. Most of the slaves worked in households or as skilled laborers in manufacturing shops and other businesses around Little Rock. The entire city was serviced by a gas system that allowed residents to illuminate their homes and business. Five schools served the city, along with four newspapers, fourteen manufacturing plants, and numerous other businesses. The city was considered to be located in a healthy location, avoiding any major outbreaks of illness, and fourteen doctors served the residents. But the city also stood apart from the other settlements scattered across the state for other reasons. The slaves who resided in the city were unlike the men and women kept in bondage across the heavily agricultural areas in the eastern and southern parts of the state. With an economy based on small manufacturing operations and merchants, the use of large numbers of slaves for agricultural operations was not required. No free blacks resided in the city, likely due in part to the passage of Act 151 by the Arkansas legislature in 1859. This law called for all free blacks in the state to depart or face enslavement for one year. The proceeds from their labor during this time would be used to pay for the former freeman's removal from the borders of Arkansas. There is little evidence that this law was ever enforced, but the threat of enslavement did force most of the free blacks who lived across the state to migrate. An estimated 700 free blacks lived in the state before the passage of Act 151, but only 144 remained to be counted in the 1860 census.[63]

The people of the city had little in common with many of their fellow Arkansans. While slavery played an important role in both their daily lives and in the economy of the city, the entire well being of the white population did not rest on the use of slaves efficiently bringing in a crop. At the same time, many of the volunteers congregating in Little Rock came from communities that were completely dependent on the institution of slavery for their current and future financial success. This vested interest in the continued existence of slavery made these two groups see the election of Lincoln in a different light. Many of the citizens in Little Rock did not wish to leave the Union and supported a cautious approach to the question of secession. Rather than acting rashly and immediately leaving the Union on the election of Lincoln, the majority of people in Little Rock wished to see what the inauguration of the new president would bring. Most of the men who had descended on the city to help capture the arsenal were of the opinion that Arkansas should not risk remaining in the Union under the leadership that would shortly take office. Instead, these men believed that Arkansas should take this opportunity to strike out and assert its independence from the Federal government.

The Capitol Guards marched from Captain Peay's home to the grounds of the statehouse, where most of the militia men from around the state encamped. Rather than setting up a perimeter around the arsenal to protect it from attack, the Capitol Guards instead surrounded the other militia units to prevent them from leaving the area and marching on the arsenal, which was located about a mile away. These actions were not warmly received by the now encircled militia troops, who responded with catcalls and other verbal abuse directed toward the Capitol Guards.[64]

The citizens of Little Rock now saw the events transpiring in their city growing more desperate by the minute. With the introduction of the Capitol Guards to the quickly growing situation, many citizens of the city knew that they had to act quickly to prevent bloodshed in their streets. The city council had passed several resolutions that had not remedied the situation but rather worked to further inflame tensions. It would be up to the common citizens of the city to put an end to the crisis. A spontaneous citizens' meeting was held in the streets near the statehouse, and almost one hundred men from across the city attended. The gathered citizens agreed that if the arsenal was to be taken, the action needed to be undertaken by trained soldiers and led by the elected government of the state and not a motley collection of armed men from across Arkansas. The citizens selected a delegation to visit the governor and press him to demand the surrender of the arsenal to state forces under the command of state officers. This would keep the militia units out of the fray, secure the weapons for Arkansas, nullify the reason for the Federal troops to be in the city and, most importantly of all, avoid any potential bloodshed in the streets. The request from the citizens of the city was in stark contrast with the resolution passed the day before by the city council, which openly called for the governor to organize an attack on the arsenal to take the weapons by force. A surrender by Totten according to the wishes of the citizens of the city would make such a show of force unnecessary.[65]

Rector responded to the delegation with a "promise that he would take definitive action to neutralize the arsenal within a matter of days." The governor now knew that he had the support, albeit somewhat tepid, of the citizens of Little Rock. By initially refusing to take open command or responsibility for the troops arriving in the city until this point in the crisis, Rector forced the people to Little Rock to reluctantly accept the necessity of taking the arsenal, even if only to protect their own lives and property from potential destruction. With this support from the people of Little Rock, Rector and Adjutant Burgevin called on former governor John Selden Roane to take active command of the militia troops. By calling the former governor into service, Rector accomplished two tasks. First, he finally publically accepted his responsibility in the arrival of these troops in Little Rock. By appointing Roane to command, Rector could no longer claim to not any have authority over these men. Secondly, the governor made the situation between the Capitol Guards and the other militia units potentially more explosive. Roane was not only the former governor but also the former lieutenant colonel of the Arkansas Regiment during the Mexican-American War and had fought a duel with Albert Pike, the former commander of the Capitol Guards.[66]

John Roane, like Rector, was not part of "the Family," the interrelated Democrats who ruled the state for most of its early years. Roane had been born in Tennessee and moved to Arkansas in 1837 to live with his brother in Pine Bluff and study law. Elected as a prosecuting attorney in 1840, two years later, Roane was elected to the state legislature as a Democrat. In 1844, Roane returned for a second term in the legislature and also served as speaker. Instead of returning for a third term in 1846, he formed a company of cavalry to serve in the Mexican War and joined the Arkansas Regiment at Washington, along with the Capitol Guards. Elected as the lieutenant colonel, Roane's experiences during the war were not especially outstanding and were capped off by his duel with Pike. After the war, Roane returned to Pine Bluff and practiced law while running a plantation. In 1849, Governor Thomas Drew resigned when his pay as chief executive was not raised after being elected to a second term. Roane was selected as the candidate of the Democratic Party for a special election when no organized opposition to him emerged at the party convention. He barely won the election, with less than 150 votes over the Whig candidate, and took office in early 1849. Roane's single term in office was unproductive as he clashed with the legislature on multiple issues, most notably over ideas to increase revenue. Due to the failure of both the State Bank and the Arkansas Real Estate Bank before

Roane's term as governor, the state government's credit was ruined. Roane planned to use the sale of Federal lands turned back to the state to increase revenue, but this proposal was ignored by the legislature, which instead used the money on pet projects and actually passed laws to decrease the tax base in the state, which further exacerbated the financial problems for the government of Arkansas. Declining to run for a second term, Roane left office in 1852 and returned to Pine Bluff, where he resumed farming and married in 1855.[67]

Returning to Little Rock to take command of the militia troops, former Governor Roane met with Governor Rector. Roane's experiences as the chief executive in the state mirrored what Rector was currently experiencing with the legislature. Both men struggled to work with the body, but Rector was seeing more success in pushing his secession agenda. This success came not from a willingness of the legislature to work with the governor but rather a bypassing of that body to force the secession issue in the streets surrounding the arsenal.

Totten continued to watch these actions and became more desperate as the hours passed. He sent another telegraph to Washington on February 6, writing, "Companies of armed citizens from various sections of this State have already arrived, and it is said there will soon be five thousand here for the express purpose of taking this arsenal. Instructions are urgently and immediately asked." Totten knew that the situation was quickly spiraling out of control, and unless orders arrived from Colonel Cooper, the long-awaited war might begin in the streets of Little Rock.[68]

Governor Rector meanwhile kept his promise to the citizens of the city and prepared to take definitive action against the arsenal. With Roane in charge, Rector ordered the two companies from Helena to move to the arsenal grounds. These units were selected as they were deemed to be the most orderly of the assembled secessionist forces. The two companies moved past the Capitol Guards, who were now powerless to stop them. With Rector taking responsibility of the troops and with Roane taking field command of the units, the assembled units were no longer an armed mob but rather a military force acting on the orders of the governor. When the companies arrived at the arsenal, they quickly surrounded the post and waited for the situation to unfold.[69]

Rector composed another letter to Totten, and General Thomas Merrick of the First Division, Arkansas Militia, delivered the note and waited with his staff to take the captain's reply to the governor. Rector's letter read in part "a considerable number of citizens…have come here, under arms, with the avowed purpose of taking possession of the U.S. Arsenal," and "a large force of citizens are on the march to this place for the same purpose." Continuing, the governor claimed that the movement was not authorized by him, but in an effort to "prevent a collision between the people of the State and the Federal troops," he would use his official authority to take control of the situation.[70]

After explaining the situation to Totten, Rector's letter continued with the formal demand for the surrender of the arsenal. The terms of the surrender would place the arsenal and its weapons under the authority of the state until the secession convention was potentially held on March 4. This surrender was the only solution that could "possibly prevent the effusion of blood and the destruction of the property of the citizens and the Government." Notably missing from the initial demand for surrender from the governor is any mention of the disposition of the Federal troops guarding the arsenal. Rector continued by assuring Totten that this demand was not based on the officer's personal actions but rather the situation that currently existed between the Federal government and some citizens of the southern states.[71]

With the delivery of the surrender demand, Totten knew that his situation was completely untenable. His tiny garrison was already greatly outnumbered by the volunteers in the city, and the possible arrival of even more men made the chance of a battle lopsided in favor of the enemy. While the Federal troops at the arsenal were much better armed than their opponents, Totten knew that it would be impossible to defend the arsenal without causing at least some civilian deaths or property damage. This knowledge was particularly important to him as his family and friends would likely be among those affected by any outbreak of violence. In the days leading up to the receipt of the surrender demand, private citizens from across the city visited Totten at the arsenal. Many pleaded with him to avoid any chance of bloodshed and simply and peacefully surrender the post. Second Lieutenant St. Clair Dearing also advised Totten to surrender to the state authorities to prevent possible violence. However, Dearing's motivations at this moment might be suspect as he was a native of Georgia and after the secession of his home state, the officer tendered his resignation. It had not yet been accepted by the War Department in Washington, and he continued to perform his duties at the arsenal, but there is no evidence that 1st Lieutenant Anderson Merchant similarly advised Totten to surrender the post.[72]

At this point, Totten knew that the situation was lost. Not only did he face the volunteer troops surrounding the post, but he also did not have the support of the people of Little Rock and at least one of his fellow officers, and most importantly, he had yet to receive any orders from Washington. With this information, Totten knew that surrender was the only option. However, the question of the treatment he and his men would receive if they surrendered was still unresolved. Totten's reply to Rector covered this topic, as well as other details concerning the surrender.

Written the same day he received the surrender demand from Rector, Totten's reply queried the governor about the specifics of the surrender. The first point Totten raised was the responsibility of the munitions held at the arsenal. While Rector demanded that the arsenal and its weapons be surrendered to state authorities and be used as Arkansas saw fit after the proposed secession convention was held on March 4, Totten asked the governor if he would "officially take charge of…arsenal and munitions of war in the name of the United States Government, and hold them in that light until future circumstances shall legally absolve him of the responsibility?" Totten continued, asking that he and his men be allowed to leave the state in any direction that he chose and that the men would be allowed to take all individual and private property, as well as any government property that they brought to the post or had been delivered during their stay in Little Rock. Finally, the captain asked that he and his men be allowed to honorably leave the arsenal. On this point, Totten emphasized that he and his men would only leave their posts "for want of instructions from their superiors in office." With that in mind, he requested that the Federal soldiers be allowed to march from the arsenal at 3:00 p.m. on February 7, and the governor would then take charge of the facility.[73]

As these messages were being passed between Rector and Totten, other elected officials from Arkansas were watching the unfolding events in horror. While other states had taken the forts and other military posts within their borders, these actions were conducted by states that were no longer part of the Union. Arkansas was still very much a member of the Union and would not even hold a vote to decide if it would remain in the United States for more than a week. Both senators from the state, Robert Ward Johnson and William King Sebastian, telegraphed Rector, telling him, "The motives which impelled capture of forts in other States do not exist in ours. It is all premature."[74] Another telegraph sent on the same day from Johnson read in part, "If Totten resists, for God's sake deliberate and go stop the assault."[75] Albert Pike also wrote from Washington that an attack would only complicate matters, and "the reasons that existed elsewhere for seizure do not exist with us."[76] All of the communications from the nation's capital implored Rector and others on the scene to act cautiously. Representative

Hindman and Senator Johnson sent Rector another telegraph on February 8. This communication did not ask Rector to stop the expected assault but rather to not "attack the arsenal unless success is certain. Repulse would be disgraceful."[77] By this point, however, the situation was almost resolved.

Rector knew that he would not be able to get better terms from Totten, and the governor quickly accepted the captain's proposal. Writing on February 7, Rector agreed to all three of Totten's proposals with some clarification. Even though most of the soldiers guarding the arsenal were artillerymen, Battery F did not bring any cannons with it from Fort Smith. Although four guns were at the arsenal, these weapons had been placed there previously. Rector demanded that these weapons stay at the post and said that only items that the troops brought with them from Fort Smith would be allowed to be taken from the arsenal.[78]

Totten agreed with these terms and ordered Lieutenant Dearing to prepare new orders for the enlisted men. Another message passed from Rector to Totten with the specifics of the handover of the facility. By 12:00 p.m. on February 8, the entire arsenal would be passed into the hands of state authorities, but the soldiers would have as long as they needed to remove their personal items from the post. On February 8, the soldiers were informed at their morning assembly that they would be departing the arsenal and would move into a camp on the banks of the Arkansas River.[79]

Officers of the militia units joined the Federal officers at the post to complete an updated inventory of the weapons and other items that would remain at the arsenal while the final agreement between Totten and Rector was drafted. Four copies were eventually created, and the two men signed each copy. The final document contained copies of Rector's demand for the surrender of the arsenal, Totten's response to that demand and finally the response of Rector receiving the captain's surrender. Attached to these papers was a memorandum that described the situation. It read in part that Totten surrendered in the face of an overwhelming armed force that was likely to shortly be reinforced and to prevent an assault that would likely lead to the sacrifice of his command. The document continued, detailing the impact that such an assault would have on the citizens and property in the city and the fact that Totten did not have any additional orders from his superiors. Finally, the memorandum detailed that Totten "took, of necessity, the responsibility of doing what he thought proper and best under all the circumstances, desiring to avoid cause of civil war in this Government, by the first instance of hostile and bloody collision." It closed by placing the blame for the situation not on Totten but rather the current government in Washington.[80]

After each copy of the surrender document was signed, the official handover of the arsenal was complete. The entire complement of Federal troops stood in formation on the post's parade ground, as did the Capitol Guards. Totten took command of his men, and they began to march away from the arsenal. The Capitol Guards escorted the Federal troops to protect them from any outburst of violence emanating from the civilians and the other volunteer units that lined the route. Marching toward the Arkansas River, the troops turned onto the Pine Bluff Road that led to the southeast, following the riverbank. After a march of seven miles, the Federals halted at Fletcher's Landing, where they set up camp. It was impossible for Totten to immediately lead his men out of the state. The situation escalated too quickly to arrange for any transportation, and the troops would remain at the landing until a boat could be dispatched to pick them up. Fletcher's Landing was selected as an appropriate location as it was well removed from the city and the volunteer militia members who remained in the area.[81]

As the men worked to construct their camp, Totten continued to work on reports for his superiors in Washington. This was the first time that the captain mentioned to Colonel Cooper that he had actually been forced to surrender the arsenal. All previous communications from Totten were written before he reached the final decision to abandon the post. Totten clearly felt that he was forced to surrender due to the lack of leadership from Washington. By avoiding bloodshed, the officer believed "in the absence of all instructions, I have only done what appears to be the course indicated by the present administration in its past course, so far as I am informed." Totten also noted that the majority of the citizens of Little Rock did not support the governor's actions and, in fact, were opposed to any action taken against the arsenal.[82]

With the Federal troops out of the city, a group of 107 women from across the city paid tribute to Totten and praised him for avoiding any bloodshed on their streets. Totten accepted an engraved sword from the women. The weapon read, "To Capt. James Totten, from the ladies of Little Rock," on one side and the other read "When woman suffers, chivalry forbears; The soldier fears all danger but his own." The note that accompanied the gift closed with a request, "Accept this tribute of our respect and gratitude, wear it in defence of your country, but sooner let it rust in your scabbard, than draw it in the cause of injustice or oppression." After accepting the sword, Totten replied, saying in part "it shall be borne in the defence of my country always, when right, and never in any land or against any people on the side of wrong, injustice, oppression, or their constitutional rights."[83]

The Federal troops remained in camp at Fletcher's Landing until February 12, when the steamboat *Madora* arrived to transport the men out of Arkansas. Steaming to the Jefferson Barracks located outside of St. Louis, Missouri, Totten and his men arrived on February 22. With the departure of the Federals from the state, the Little Rock Arsenal crisis could finally be deemed to be over.[84]

Although the threat of violence in the streets of Little Rock had passed, the actions of Governor Rector and the volunteer militia units pushed Arkansas to answer the secession question. With control of the arsenal, Rector could now ensure that those weapons would not be used against Arkansans, even though the current presidential administration had not displayed any evidence that such an action was likely or even possible. Instead of solidifying the state behind the small pro-secessionist faction that existed in the eastern and southern areas of the state, Rector's actions pushed more people to realize that disunion would only lead to the possibility of violence. Now the governor and the other secessionists in the state would need the support of the people to call for a convention to formally begin the process of leaving the Union.

Chapter 5

Arkansas Leaves the Union

With the surrender of the arsenal by Captain Totten and his Federal troops, most of the citizens of Little Rock felt that the crisis had passed and life would return to normal, at least until the statewide vote on secession was held later that month. The voters of the state visited the polls on February 18, and the final tally revealed that 27,412 voted to hold a secession convention with another 15,826 against the proposition. While a majority of voters did want a convention to answer the question about Arkansas's future in the Union, pro-unionist delegates received almost 6,000 more votes than their secessionist counterparts. The final count revealed that the majority of voters in the state were unsure about the prospect of leaving the Union, although the actions undertaken at Little Rock seemed to indicate that the Federal government was an unwelcome intrusion in the affairs of the state.[85]

The secession convention finally met on March 4 in Little Rock and the Unionist sentiments among the delegates continued to be apparent with the election of David Walker of Fayetteville as the convention president. Walker was an avowed Unionist and led the group in rejecting immediate secession. Rather, after more than two weeks of debate, the convention called for the question to be put before the voters of the state again. A referendum was scheduled for August to allow the citizens of the state to determine by a simple majority if Arkansas would continue her association with the Federal government. With a possible solution in sight, the convention adjourned and returned home. However, events both inside and outside of the state would eventually preempt the vote.[86]

After the secession convention met and Arkansas remained in the Union for the time being, the seizure of Federal military property across the state continued. At the time of the seizure of the Little Rock Arsenal, Fort Smith was still manned by a small number of Federal troops. A shipment of munitions destined for Fort Smith and other posts in the Indian Territory was "seized by certain individuals pretending to act for the State of Arkansas," according to a report by Major Justus McKinstry. These items were being transported up the Mississippi River and entered the mouth of the Arkansas River near Napoleon, Arkansas. Shipped on the steamship *Southwester*, the inventory taken included forty thousand rifle cartridges, fifty thousand pistol cartridges, twenty thousand blank cartridges and other items. A second shipment on the steamship *Sunshine* captured at the same time included enough cavalry equipment to outfit eighty-three horses.[87]

By April, the seizure of Federal military property was becoming quite common in the state. State commissioners in charge of the defense of Arkansas, including future Confederate major general Thomas James Churchill, ordered a shipment of weapons from Cincinnati, Ohio. These weapons would be used to arm any troops from the state in case of war. Due to the quickly changing situation across the South, including the secession of Mississippi and Louisiana, the weapons were never delivered, as their safety could not be guaranteed. Pro-secessionist groups in eastern Arkansas responded by capturing any ship carrying military goods that belonged to the national government. These actions put the Federal posts at Fort Smith and the Indian Territory in a precarious situation, as they each relied on the stream of supplies that typically flowed up the Arkansas.[88]

Not only were events in Arkansas continuing to spiral out of control, but also open war between the seceded states and the Federal government finally broke out. Military forces in South Carolina fired on Fort Sumter on April 12, prompting President Lincoln to call for troops to help restore order. As a member of the Union, Arkansas was asked to contribute 780 men. Governor Rector refused, saying "the people of this commonwealth are freemen, not slaves and will defend to the last extremity their honor, lives and property against Northern mendacity and usurpation." While it was still unclear if Arkansas would officially leave the United States, rhetoric from the chief executive of the state made that likelihood very remote.[89]

Even as news of these events in the eastern part of the country reached Arkansas, people across the state continued to make military preparations. The rumors of the capture of vessels carrying Federal military supplies traveled upriver to the garrison at Fort Smith. Captain William Burns was dispatched from the fort to steam down the Arkansas River to determine the true situation. Arriving in Little Rock on April 20, the officer found that preparations were being made in the capital to stop boats with military supplies. Burns reported that a steamboat called the *Sky Lark* had been stopped and searched and all military stores removed before it was allowed to resume its journey up the river. Anxious to prevent similar situations, Burns tried to meet with Governor Rector but was unable to do so. Other events in Little Rock also alarmed the officer. He noted groups of men organizing to capture the military post at Fort Smith, and the steamboat on which he traveled down the Arkansas was chartered to carry these men upriver. Continuing down the river to Pine Bluff, Burns found the *Silver Lake Number 2* guarded by a number of armed men. This steamboat had been carrying Federal military supplies, which were now under the command of a Mr. Bell. Burns was unable to determine how Bell was in charge but suspected that he was an agent of the governor and was tasked with transporting the supplies taken from the *Silver Lake* to Little Rock. Rather than return to Fort Smith during a possible assault, Burns instead traveled to St. Louis to meet with Colonel William Emory to organize a supply effort to reach Fort Washita in the Indian Territory.[90]

As the situation continued to deteriorate, the Federal army decided to abandon all the military posts in the Indian Territory on April 17. These three major posts, named Forts Arbuckle, Cobb and Washita, were evacuated over the next two weeks, and the men posted at the facilities moved northward into Kansas to Forts Leavenworth and Scott. The War Department thought that Arkansas volunteers might move into the area to garrison the forts, but the commanders of each post were ordered not to wait for the arrival of these troops and instead to complete their evacuation as quickly as possible. Some southern troops did move into the area. The last group of Federal soldiers to depart Fort Arbuckle was captured by a unit of Texas troops who moved into the area to seize any military supplies that might remain after the evacuation.[91]

On April 23, the last Federal forces also departed Fort Smith. This withdrawal left the Indian Territory completely unguarded except for the occasional unit of Texas State Troops. Only two companies of cavalry were stationed at the post under the command of Major Samuel Sturgis, who decided to evacuate the fort under the cover of night before marching into the Indian Territory en route to safety in Kansas. Sturgis was forced to leave the sick, the hospital steward, laundresses and others who could not quickly travel behind at the fort. Shortly after the departure of the troops, a force of volunteer Arkansas troops arrived at the fort to take it in the name of Governor Rector. Under the command of Solon Borland, former senator and major of the Arkansas Regiment during the Mexican War, the Arkansas troops numbered around 235 men and a battery of artillery. It is unclear but likely that these cannon and other weapons were taken from the arsenal at Little Rock. Steaming up the Arkansas River on the *Frederick Notrebe* and *Tahlequah*, the command was cheered by civilians on the riverbank and joined by other volunteers while en route to the post. Disappointed to find the post mostly evacuated, the Arkansans consoled themselves by taking the few remaining Federals prisoner. This included Captain Alexander Montgomery, the assistant quartermaster who had been tasked with completing the evacuation, as well as Major Richard Gatlin of the Fifth United States Infantry, who had been visiting the post. Both men were paroled after they gave their word that they would not fight against either the state of Arkansas or the "Southern Confederate States" until they were properly exchanged. While Arkansas had not officially left the Union, the state was acting as if it was already in a state of open rebellion by "capturing" Federal soldiers and demanding an oath from these men before they would be released. With these actions, Arkansas all but officially cast its lot with the Confederacy.[92]

Rector soon received word that Federal forces in the Indian Territory had been tasked with retaking Fort Smith, and he quickly acted to ensure that that did not happen. Under his orders, several units of Arkansas State Troops were posted at the fort to protect it from the expected Federal assault.[93]

Pressure continued to mount on Walker after the firing on Fort Sumter and Lincoln's call for troops, and the convention president finally called for the convention to reconvene on May 6. Some Unionist delegates argued that the state should remain committed to its timetable for the referendum in August, but this idea was quickly defeated. Secessionist delegates responded by calling for the immediate severing of all ties with the United States. The initial vote on the issue found the vast majority of delegates in favor but with five Unionist representatives still against the measure. Walker pleaded with the men to change their votes to allow the state to leave the Union on a unanimous note. Addressing the men, he said "Now, since we must go, let us all go together; let the wires carry the news to all the world that Arkansas stands as a unit against coercion." Four of the delegates did change their votes, but Isaac Murphy of Madison County refused to do so. He addressed the assembly, saying, "I have cast my vote after mature reflection, and have duly considered the consequences, and I cannot conscientiously change it."

Trapnall Hall. *Photo courtesy of the Library of Congress.*

Threats, hisses and boos were hurled at Murphy, but the entire hall quieted when Mrs. Fredrick Trapnall, a well-respected widow in the community, tossed the Unionist a bouquet. The final vote was taken at ten minutes past four in the afternoon, and Arkansas finally officially left the Union. The process of secession, which had begun in earnest with the seizure of the Little Rock Arsenal, was finally complete.[94]

Conclusion

The crisis was finally over. The men of the Second United States Artillery would soon become involved in the growing turmoil in Missouri and would help keep that state in the Union. Many of the major players in the arsenal crisis would play important roles in the war that began after the end of the crisis.

Henry Rector continued to serve as governor through the secession conventions. After the second convention approved the separation of Arkansas from the rest of the Union on May 6, the delegates remained in Little Rock to write a new constitution for the state. Confusion reigned as it became unclear who was technically in charge of the state: Rector or the convention. Eventually, Rector was able to exert his authority, but the convention responded by including in the new constitution a call for an election to be held in October 1862. This would cut Rector's current term by two years. After leading Arkansas out of the Union and through the first year of the war, Rector was defeated in his reelection bid by Harris Flanagin of Arkadelphia, who was then serving as the colonel of the Second Arkansas Mounted Rifles with the Confederate army in Tennessee. Rector received only 7,419 votes to Flanagin's 18,187. After the election, Rector resigned eleven days before the official end of his term and, after his request for a commission in the Confederate army was rejected, spent the remainder of the war in the state reserve corps. After the war, Rector returned to farming and hauling cotton, while also serving as a delegate to the 1874 Constitutional Convention. He died in Little Rock on August 12, 1899.[95]

James Totten led his battery during the early months of the war and was involved in the action at Camp Jackson and the Battle of Wilson's Creek. Further service followed in both the Western and Trans-Mississippi Theaters, and the end of the war saw him serving as a brevet brigadier general. With the demobilization of Federal forces, Totten reverted to this regular army rank of lieutenant colonel and retired in 1870. He died the next year in Sedalia, Missouri.[96]

Patrick Cleburne returned to Helena but soon joined the Confederate army. His company, called the "Yell Rifles," became part of the First Arkansas Infantry, and Cleburne was elected as the colonel of the regiment. Promoted to brigadier general in March 1862, Cleburne led a brigade at the Battles of Shiloh and Richmond, Kentucky, where he was wounded. Returning to the field in October 1862, he commanded units at the Battle of Perryville and was promoted to the rank of major general in December. Continuing his service with the Confederate Army of Tennessee, Cleburne led a division at the battles of Murfreesboro, Chickamauga and Missionary Ridge. Receiving a citation from the Confederate Congress based on his actions at Ringgold Gap, Cleburne proposed enlisting slaves into the Confederate army and granting these selected men their freedom. Little came of this suggestion at the time, and Cleburne returned to the field, where he was killed leading his division at the Battle of Franklin on November 30, 1864. Engaged to be married later that year, Cleburne's body was eventually returned to Helena. Cleburne County in north central Arkansas is named in the general's honor.[97]

Thomas Hindman would continue to serve Arkansas but would do so in a Confederate uniform. After failing to secure a seat in the Confederate Congress, he helped raise the Second Arkansas Infantry and was elected colonel. In September, he was promoted to brigadier general and led a brigade at the Battle of Shiloh, where he was wounded and shortly afterward promoted to major general. Transferred back to Arkansas, Hindman took command of the Confederate Department of the Trans-Mississippi. Faced with defending the state in the face of a Union invasion, Hindman declared martial law, conscripted men and burned cotton to prevent it from being captured by Federal forces. His heavy-handed tactics led to his demotion from command of the entire Trans-Mississippi to leading just the Department of Arkansas. Leaving his administrative duties behind, Hindman led a small army at the Battle of Prairie Grove but suffered a tactical defeat. He requested a transfer to another army and took command of a division in the Army of Tennessee. Wounded at the battles of Chickamauga and Kennesaw Mountain, Hindman left the army and joined his family in Texas before moving to Mexico. Returning to Helena in 1867, he led efforts to defeat Republican candidates at the ballot box and supported the enfranchisement of former slaves. He was assassinated on September 28, 1868, when an unknown assailant shot through a window of his home, and he is buried in Helena.[98]

Albert Pike's law career continued after his return from the Mexican-American War, and he spent time working on various projects including translation French law books into English and pursuing railroad ventures. A Whig, he left that party and was a Know-Nothing for a period. With Arkansas's secession, Pike was named by the convention as the state's commissioner to the Indian Territory. Subsequently, he received a commission as a brigadier general in the Confederate army and led a brigade of Indian troops at the Battle of Pea Ridge, where the troops were accused of scalping dead Federals on the field. Conflict between Hindman and Pike ultimately led to his resignation in the summer of 1862. He returned to Arkansas and was named to the state supreme court in 1864. After the war, he continued to practice law, served as a newspaper editor and continued his involvement with the Masonic lodge. He died in Washington, D.C., on April 2, 1891.[99]

David Walker supported the Confederate government in Arkansas after leading the secession commission and even served as a colonel on a military court. After the war, he served as the chief justice of the state supreme court and remained in that position until 1868, when a new constitution took effect. Rejoining the supreme court as an associate justice in 1874, he served until 1878, when he resigned due to failing health. He died the next year in Fayetteville.[100]

Isaac Murphy continued to serve in the convention after the state seceded from the Union but did not vote to accept either the new state constitution or the Confederate constitution. After the convention adjourned, Murphy returned home to Madison County, but in the face of continuing threats and the approach of a Union army, he fled to Missouri, where he served as an aide to Federal major general Samuel Curtis. Returning to Arkansas in 1863, Murphy was quickly nominated to serve as the provisional governor of the new Unionist state government. Taking office in March 1864, he led the state in ratifying the Thirteenth Amendment to the United States Constitution and supported issuing wide-scale pardons to former Confederates after the end of the war. Murphy remained governor during Reconstruction and was succeeded by Powell Clayton, a former general in the Union army. Murphy returned home to Madison County and farmed and practiced law until his death on September 8, 1882.[101]

John Selden Roane returned home to Pine Bluff after commanding the militia units in Little Rock and accepted a commission as a brigadier general in the Confederate army in March 1862. He served for several months as the ranking officer in Arkansas before being replaced by Major General Thomas Hindman and later commanded a brigade under Hindman at the Battle of Prairie Grove. Roane did not see any further action during the war and instead spent undistinguished time in detached and garrison posts in Arkansas, Louisiana and Texas. After the war, he returned home to Pine Bluff, where he died on April 8, 1867.[102]

Solon Borland's service during the capture of Fort Smith continued after the outbreak of war with a Confederate commission as a colonel. Posted to northeastern Arkansas, Borland began to clash with Governor Rector over a variety of topics, including the use of the state militia by Confederate commanders and an effort Borland made to control prices of essential goods. Rector complained about Borland's orders to the Confederate government in Richmond, and Secretary of War Judah Benjamin agreed with the governor. Borland soon retired from the army and returned to Little Rock to practice medicine. He moved to Dallas County before the fall of Little Rock in September 1863 and later moved to Harris County, Texas, where he died on January 1, 1864.[103]

Samuel Sturgis continued to serve in the Federal army during the Civil War. He took command at the Battle of Wilson's Creek after the death of Brigadier General Nathaniel Lyon and was later himself promoted to the rank of brigadier general. Transferred to the Eastern Theater, Sturgis led troops at the Battles of Fredericksburg and Antietam before being posted to the Western Theater. At the Battle of Brice's Cross Roads in Mississippi, Sturgis was routed by Confederate forces under the command of Lieutenant General Nathan Bedford Forrest. After this defeat, Sturgis was removed from field command. At the end of the war, he was brevetted to the rank of major general of volunteers but reverted to his permanent rank of lieutenant colonel in the regular army. Given command of the Seventh Cavalry in 1869, Sturgis was promoted to colonel and led the unit in actions against Indians. After part of the regiment was destroyed at the Battle of Little Big Horn while under the command of its lieutenant colonel, George Armstrong Custer, Sturgis led the unit in a campaign against the Nez Perce. He retired in 1886 and died in St. Paul, Minnesota, in 1889. Sturgis, South Dakota, is named in his honor.[104]

The Capitol Guards became part of Company A of the Sixth Arkansas Infantry in June 1861. The regiment marched to Pocahontas, Arkansas, and

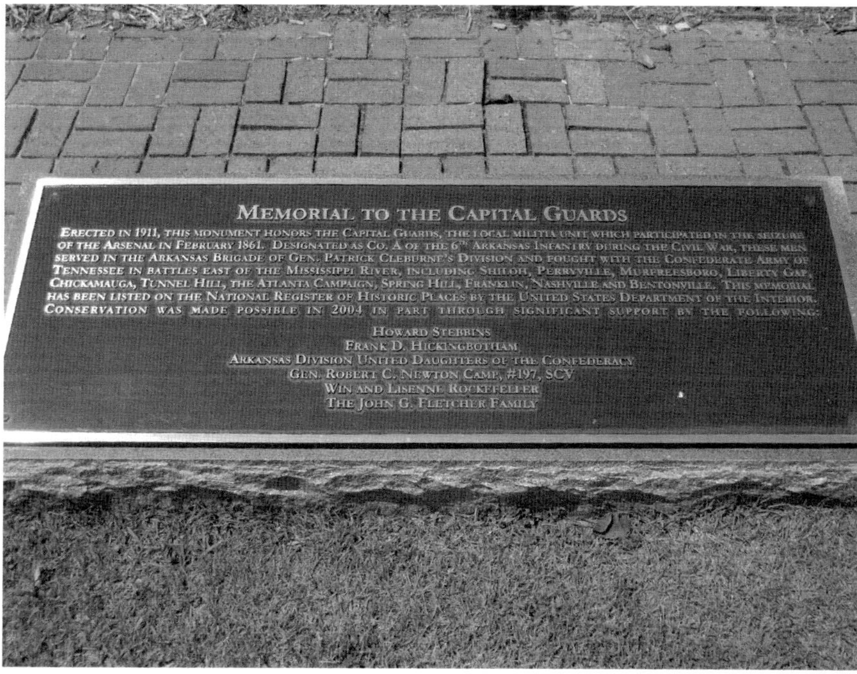

Memorial to the Capital Guards. *Photo by David Sesser.*

joined a brigade with four other Arkansas regiments. Moving across the Mississippi River, the unit saw action in Kentucky and served in Hindman at the Battle of Shiloh. The Sixth next saw action at the Battle of Perryville, and in response to the number of casualties suffered by the unit, the regiment was consolidated with the Seventh Arkansas Infantry. Service at the battles of Murfreesboro, Chickamauga and the Atlanta Campaign followed. The entire brigade was captured at the Battle of Jonesboro near Atlanta. Quickly exchanged, the unit next saw action at Spring Hill, Franklin and Nashville. Eventually, the original unit was consolidated with ten other regiments to form the First Arkansas Consolidated Infantry, which surrendered with the Army of Tennessee on April 29, 1865. Only a handful of men from the original Capitol Guards were present due to the extreme losses that the company had suffered from four years of war. The unit was not reformed after the war, but by 1881, a new unit called the Capital City Guards had been established.[105]

After the Arkansas volunteers under the command of Solon Borland took control of Fort Smith, they were reinforced by thousands of other Arkansans eager to join in the fight. These men were eventually replaced by a unit of the Arkansas militia, who were in turn replaced by regular Confederate troops. As a gateway to the Indian Territory to the west and a supply and organizational post for Confederate actions in northwest Arkansas, the fort was an important post for the southern forces. The fort served as the headquarters of Albert Pike, named as the commissioner to negotiate treaties with the Five Civilized Tribes in the Indian Territory. Eventually falling to Federal forces on September 1, 1863, the fort remained in Union hands for the remainder of the war. The post was decommissioned in 1871, and the United States District Court for the Western District of Arkansas, which also served the nearby Indian Territory, was moved to the fort. During this period, the population of the city surrounding the fort exploded as the settlement grew into an important regional center. The city of Fort Smith eventually took control of the site of the military post, and in 1964, it was added to the National Park Service.[106]

The Little Rock Arsenal remained in the hands of the state for several months. After Arkansas officially seceded from the Union on May 6, the state joined the Confederate States of America on May 18. Three days later, control of the arsenal and Fort Smith passed to the Confederate government. Most of the weapons held at the arsenal were issued to Arkansas units shortly after the transfer was complete. Parts of the Fifth, Sixth, Seventh, Eighth, Ninth and Tenth Arkansas Infantry Regiments received flintlocks from the stores held at the arsenal. The Third Arkansas Cavalry also received weapons from the arsenal.[107]

The arsenal most notably supplied a unit that called itself the Totten Battery, named in honor of the Federal officer who avoided bloodshed in the streets of Little Rock. Eventually, the name of the unit was changed to the Pulaski Light Artillery, and it served under Captain William Woodruff, the son of the editor of the *Arkansas Gazette*. At the Battle of Wilson's Creek, one of the officers of the unit, Lieutenant Omer Weaver, became the first Arkansan to die in the war when he was struck by artillery fire from a battery under the command of James Totten. The Pulaski Light Artillery changed its name again to honor the young officer and continued to serve in the Trans-Mississippi Theater as the Weaver Light Artillery.[108]

Opposite, top: Modern Fort Smith Commissary. *Photo by David Sesser.*

Opposite, bottom: Gallows at Fort Smith. *Photo by David Sesser.*

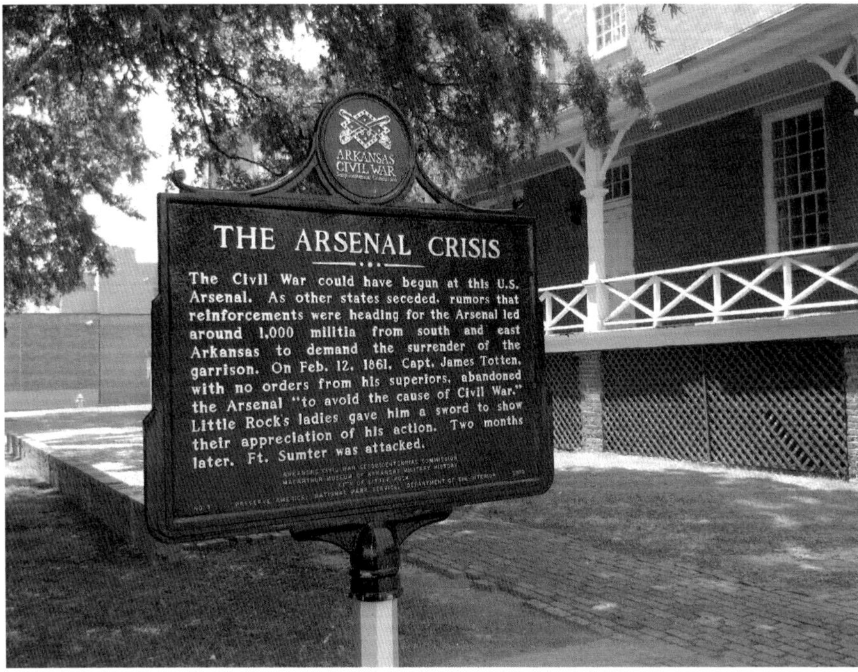

Above: Historical marker detailing the events of the arsenal crisis. *Photo by David Sesser*.

Left: Lieutenant Omer Weaver of the Pulaski Light Artillery, originally named the Totten Light Artillery in honor of Captain James Totten and his father. Weaver was killed at the Battle of Wilson's Creek while facing a Union battery under the command of Captain Totten. Weaver, Omer R. WICR 30810 in the collection of Wilson's Creek National Battlefield. *Image courtesy of the National Park Service.*

Major General Frederick Steele. *Photo courtesy of the Library of Congress.*

After the fall of Little Rock to Federal forces in September 1863, under the command of Major General Frederick Steele, the arsenal was used by the occupying forces. When seventeen-year-old David Owen Dodd was arrested by Federal forces for spying in December 1863, he was taken to the arsenal. After a trial, he was convicted and hanged on the grounds of St. John's College just east of the arsenal grounds on January 8, 1864.[109]

After the war ended, the post remained under the control of the United States Army, which continued to utilize and update the arsenal and its grounds. In 1868, porches that can still be seen today were added to both the front and rear of the Tower Building. In light of the changing

Union Soldiers in Little Rock. *Photo courtesy of the Library of Congress.*

BANKING OFFICE

General Douglas MacArthur. *Photo courtesy of the Library of Congress.*

Opposite: MacArthur Memorial on the grounds of the arsenal. *Photo by David Sesser.*

mission of the post, it was renamed the Little Rock Barracks in 1873. Soldiers continued to be posted at the barracks, including Captain Arthur MacArthur, recipient of the Medal of Honor for actions during the Civil War. MacArthur's youngest son was born at the post on January 26, 1880, and he would also later earn the Medal of Honor. General of the Army Douglas MacArthur received the medal for his actions during the Philippines Campaign in 1941–42. MacArthur would go on to recapture the Philippines and lead the Allied forces to victory in the Pacific Theater during the Second World War.[110]

The continued growth of Little Rock led the city and the Federal government to swap the post for one thousand undeveloped acres in 1892. As part of the swap, the city agreed to use the grounds exclusively as a public park. In 1911, the grounds were used for a reunion of Confederate veterans, and the same year, a statue was dedicated in front of the Tower Building to the Capitol Guards. As the years passed, most of the buildings on the arsenal grounds were removed until only the Tower building remained standing, and it eventually fell into disrepair. In 1939, the building was restored, and in 1942, the Museum of Science and Natural History opened in the facility. Additional remodels and renovations also occurred in 1959, 1965 and 1992.

Above: Modern arsenal building. The building on the far right is the Arkansas Arts Center. *Photo by David Sesser.*

Top: Modern rear of the arsenal building. *Photo by David Sesser.*

Opposite, top: Rear of the arsenal building in the early twentieth century when the area served as a city park.

Opposite, bottom: Capital Guards Monument at the arsenal. *Photo by David Sesser.*

In 1959, the Arkansas Arts Center was opened next to the Tower Building on ground that formerly belonged to the arsenal. In 1995, the City of Little Rock Board of Directors created the MacArthur Military History Museum Commission, which led to the creation of a military museum in the Tower Building. The Museum of Science and Natural History moved to a new location several blocks away, and the MacArthur Museum of Arkansas Military History opened in 2001. Named for the general of the army who was born in the building, the museum continues to operate in this location and plays an important role in preserving the expansive military heritage of Arkansas and its citizens.[111]

The crisis that occurred in Little Rock in early 1861 almost led to violence in the streets and the possibility that the Civil War would have begun in Arkansas. Eventually, cooler heads prevailed, and thankfully Little Rock did not become known as the place where the war started.

Appendix A

Timeline of Events Relating to the Little Rock Arsenal Crisis

1817: Military forces construct the first Fort Smith.

June 15, 1836: Arkansas is admitted to the Union as the twenty-fifth state and the thirteenth slave state.

1837: Land for the Little Rock Arsenal is purchased.

May 1838: Construction of the arsenal begins.

1838: A permanent post is constructed and manned at Fort Smith after years of lobbying by the citizens of the area.

November 6, 1860: Abraham Lincoln of the Republican Party is elected as the sixteenth president of the United States; John C. Breckinridge, representing the Southern Democrats, wins Arkansas. Henry Rector is elected as the sixth governor of Arkansas.

November 21, 1860: Battery F, Second United States Artillery, under the command of Captain James Totten, is ordered from Fort Smith to garrison the Little Rock Arsenal.

November 27, 1860: Battery F departs Fort Smith.

December 6, 1860: Battery F arrives in Little Rock and takes its post at the arsenal.

DECEMBER 20, 1860: South Carolina becomes the first southern state to leave the Union.

DECEMBER 22, 1860: Arkansas House of Representatives approves a measure that would allow voters to determine to hold a convention to meet on the issue of secession and to elect representatives to that convention.

JANUARY 16, 1861: Arkansas State Senate approves a call for a public referendum on the question of a secession convention.

JANUARY 28, 1861: Governor Rector informs Captain James Totten that the people of Arkansas own the weapons in the arsenal and would shortly decide whether or not to remain in the Union.

FEBRUARY 6, 1861: The Little Rock City Council calls out the Capitol Guards to keep the peace between the militia units from around the state and the Federal troops at the arsenal.

FEBRUARY 6, 1861: Governor Rector calls on Captain Totten to surrender the arsenal.

FEBRUARY 7, 1861: Totten and Rector come to terms over the surrender of the post.

FEBRUARY 8, 1861: The arsenal surrenders, and control passes to the state.

FEBRUARY 12, 1861: Totten and his men depart from Fletcher's Landing.

FEBRUARY 18, 1861: Voters in Arkansas support a call for a secession convention.

FEBRUARY 22, 1861: The Federal troops from the arsenal arrive in St. Louis.

MARCH 4, 1861: First secession convention is held in the state.

MARCH 4, 1861: Abraham Lincoln is inaugurated as the sixteenth president of the United States.

APRIL 12, 1861: Fort Sumter is fired on in Charleston, South Carolina.

APRIL 17, 1861: Forts in the Indian Territory are abandoned by the Federal army.

APRIL 22, 1861: Arkansas refuses to supply troops to the Federal government to put down the rebellion.

APRIL 23, 1861: Fort Smith is abandoned and occupied by Arkansas troops a short time later.

MAY 6, 1861: The recalled secession convention votes to leave the Union.

Appendix B

Reports and Correspondence of the Seizure of the U.S. Arsenal at Little Rock

LITTLE ROCK ARSENAL,
Little Rock, Ark., January 29, 1861.
SIR: I have the honor herewith to inclose a copy of a communication received this day from his Excellency Henry M. Rector, governor of the State of Arkansas, and also a copy of my reply to his excellency's communications.

Please submit both these communications to the Secretary of War for the decision of the President of the United States, with the request that instructions be sent me as to my future action in the premises. I also request that means and money may be sent me to carry out the orders I may receive.

I forward, in the same mail with this, copies of the communications, herein mentioned, to the general commanding the Department of the West. I deem it necessary in this connection respectfully to inform the authorities concerned that, in my opinion, most positive and unequivocal instructions are called for, in order that I may not mistake the intentions of the administration regarding the matter at issue. I believe there is trouble ahead for this command, and that by the 4th day of March coming decided action will be absolutely imperative in the officer who may than command this arsenal, and, if left to his own discretion, he may not in everything correspond with the wishes of the Federal authorities.

Whatever orders may be given, I respectfully ask that they may be sent by a reliable agent, and not by mails, as there appears to be some reason in believing that they are not entirely trustworthy at present. I would not myself, in the present instance, trust to this doubtful medium of communication if I had means at my disposal of sending an officer to Washington, and, indeed, if I can procure the necessary funds,

I may yet forward copies of the various communications now inclosed by such an agent as indicated.

I am, sir, very respectfully, your obedient servant,

JAS. TOTTEN,

Captain, Second Artillery, Commanding Post.

Colonel S. COOPER,

Adjutant-General U.S. Army, Washington City, D.C.

[Inclosure A.]

THE STATE OF ARKANSAS,

Executive Department, Little Rock, January 28, 1861.

CAPTAIN: The public exigencies require me to make known to you that the U.S. Arsenal at this place will be permitted to remain in the possession of the Federal officers until the State, by authority of the people, shall have determined to sever their connection with the General Government, unless, however, wit should be thought proper to order additional forces to this point; or, on the other hand, an attempt should be made to remove or destroy the munitions of war deposited in said arsenal.

Any assurances that you may be able to give touching the observance of these two latter conditions will greatly tend to quiet the public mind, and prevent a collision between the sovereign people of Arkansas and the Government troops now stationed at this point.

Respectfully,

HENRY M. RECTOR,

Governor of Arkansas and Commander-in-Chief.

Captain TOTTEN, U.S. Army, Little Rock Arsenal.

[Inclosure B.]

HEADQUARTERS LITTLE ROCK ARSENAL,

Little Rock, Ark., January 29, 1861.

SIR: I have to acknowledge the receipt of you communication of the 28th instant, which was handed to me this morning by your aide-de-camp, J.J. Gaines, esq., and in answer thereto, to say to your excellency that my understanding leads me to believe that the troops under my command were ordered here at the request of some of the members of Congress from this State, and several good citizens also, for what reasons, if any, I have not been apprised.

As you will readily understand, I cannot give your excellency any assurances as to what instructions may in future be issued regarding this arsenal and the Federal troops now stationed here, but I can assure you that, so far as I am informed, no orders, such as you refer to in your two propositions, have been issued, nor do I believe, privately and unofficially, that any such orders will be given by the Federal Government. I have furthermore to remind your excellency that as an officer of the Army of the United states, my allegiance is due to that Government in whose [service] I am, and that I act by its authority and permission, and until absolved from the allegiance my honor is concerned in the faithful performance of what I may conceive to be my duty.

I shall forward your communication to the Secretary of War to be laid before the President of the United States, and ask instructions relative to the matter contained in it, and, if not prohibited by these authorities, I will cheerfully inform your excellency what these instructions are.

In the mean time (*sic*) let me say, in conclusion, that I most cordially concur with your excellency in the desire to avoid collision between the Federal troops under my command and the citizens of Arkansas, and shall do everything in my power which an honorable man in my position can or dare do to prevent so deplorable an event.

I am, respectfully,
JAS. TOTTEN,
Captain, Second Artillery, U.S. Army.
His Excellency HENRY M. RECTOR,
Governor of Arkansas and Commander-in-Chief.

LITTLE ROCK, February 6, 1861.
I have to inform the authorities that companies of armed citizens from various section of this State have already arrived, and it is said there will soon be five thousand here for the express purpose of taking this arsenal. Instructions are urgently and immediately asked. Collision seems inevitable if this arsenal is to be held.
JAMES TOTTEN,
Captain, Second Artillery, Commanding Post.
Colonel S. COOPER, Adjutant-General U.S. Army.

LITTLE ROCK ARSENAL,
Little Rock, Ark., February 6, 1861.
SIR: I have the honor herewith to inclose a copy of a communication just received from H.M. Rector, governor of the State of Arkansas, demanding the surrender of this arsenal to the State authorities.

As I have already written and telegraphed you for the information of the President, I am perfectly in the dark as to the wishes of the administration, from the want [of] instructions how to meet such a crisis as at present. If I had positive orders to cover the case in point I should obey them implicitly; but I have nothing whatever, within my knowledge, indicative of the course the Government wishes its agents to pursue, and I am therefore left to act as my judgment and my honor as a Federal officer dictate under the present trying circumstances.

I inclose also copies of certain resolutions, passed by the citizens of Little Rock, and of the common council of said city, explanatory of the circumstances under which the matter above referred to had been brought about.

I am, very respectfully, your obedient servant,
JAS. TOTTEN,
Captain, Second Artillery, Commanding Post.
Colonel S. COOPER,
Adjutant-General U.S. Army, Washington, D.C.

[Inclosure A.]
EXECUTIVE OFFICE,
Little Rock, Ark., February 6, 1861.

SIR: There is now in this city a considerable number of the citizens of this State who have come here, under arms, with the avowed purpose of taking possession of the U.S. Arsenal.

Reliable information has been received that a large force of citizens are on the march to this place for the same purpose. This movement is prompted by the feeling that pervades the citizens of this State that in the present emergency the arms and monitions of war in the arsenal should be under the control of the State authorities, in order to their security. This movement, although not authorized by me, has assumed such an aspect that it becomes my duty, as the executive of this State, to interpose my official authority to prevent a collision between the people of the State and the Federal troops under your command.

I therefore demand in the name of the State the delivery of the possession of the arsenal and monitions of war under your charge to the State authorities, to be held subject to the action of the convention to be held on the 4th of March next. This course is the only one which can possibly prevent the effusion of blood and the destruction of the property of the citizens and the Government. I beg leave to assure you that the steps which the citizens have seen fit to take is not prompted by any personal distrust of you, but the jealousy which naturally exists towards the authorities of the United States under the present unhappy condition of the country.

This communication will be handed you by T.D. Merrick, general of First Division of the Arkansas Militia, who will call on you personally, accompanied by his staff, and who will receive from you your response.

Respectfully, your obedient servant,

HENRY M. RECTOR,
Governor of Arkansas.
Captain TOTTEN,
Commanding U.S. Arsenal, Little Rock, Ark.

[Indorsement]
This is the paper marked "A."
HENRY M. RECTOR,
Governor of Arkansas.
JAMES TOTTEN,
Captain, Second Artillery.

[Inclosure B.]
COUNCIL CHAMBER,
Little Rock, Ark., February 5, 1861—3 o'clock p. m.
Resolved as a sense of this council, That if there be any impending danger or necessity which requires the seizure of the U.S. Arsenal at head of the State, to order such seizure to be made by the organized military power of the State.

But that all unauthorized attempts to seize the arsenal by persons without orders from the governor is an insult to his station and authority, and deserves the reprehension of all our people, and calculated to injure the cause of States rights, and we earnestly recommend the governor to interpose his authority to check any such movements if unauthorized by him.

Resolved, That a copy of these resolution be immediately communicated to the governor, and that a committee, to consist of the whole council, be appointed for that purpose, and the same committee to communicate with the leaders of such movement.
C.P. BERTRAND,
Mayor pro tem.
Attest:
A.J. SMITH, City Recorder.

[Inclosure C.]
COUNCIL CHAMBER,
Little Rock, Ark., February, 6, 1861.
At a called meeting of the city council, held at 4 o'clock p. m. of this day—
Present: Charles P. Bertrand, mayor *pro tem.*, and Aldermen Waid, Peary, Tucker, Watkins, Henry, Robins, and George—
The following preamble and resolutions were introduced by Alderman Geo. C. Watkins:

"Whereas an armed force of about four hundred men from different parts of this State are assembled at Little Rock for the purpose of seizing the U.S. Arsenal at this place, under the apprehension that the arsenal and the arms and the munitions of war stored therein may at no distant day be used to the injury of the people of this State, and it is reasonably certain that such force will soon be increased to one thousand men, or to five thousand, if necessary for the purpose designed;

"And whereas the governor of the State has on this day officially assumed the responsibility of said movement, and has made a demand in the name and by authority of the State upon the officer in command of the arsenal to surrender the same to the authorities of the State;

"And whereas the arsenal is so located that any attack or defense of it would involve the destruction of much of the property of private citizens of Little Rock, and the loss of many lives of our citizens, and the probable sacrifice of the officers and their command in charge of the arsenal: Therefore,

"Resolved, That this council do earnestly deprecate a hostile collision in their midst between the forces of the State and the United States troops stationed at the arsenal, and hope that same may be avoided if it can possibly be done consistently with a proper sense of duty and honor on the part of those upon whom rests the responsibility of a collision and the deplorable consequences that would inevitably result from it.

"Resolved further, That a copy of these resolutions be furnished to the governor of the State, and also a copy of the same of the officer in command of the arsenal at this place."

A true copy from the record:

Attest:

GORDON W. PEARY,

Acting Recorder pro tem.

[Inclosure D.]

Whereas many good citizens of this State have come to Little Rock in obedience to what they supposed to be the orders of the governor, to assist in taking the U.S. Arsenal at this place; and whereas the governor disavows such orders as being without his authority or sanction: Therefore,

"Resolved, As the opinion of this meeting, that it is the duty of the governor to assume the responsibility of this movement or to interpose his authority and influence to prevent it.

"Resolved further, That in case there be, in opinion of the governor, any danger or necessity for seizing the arsenal, we earnestly recommend him, as the only way to prevent the effusion of blood, to order the same to be done in his official capacity and in the name and by authority of the State, and to that end that he make an official demand upon the officers in charge of the arsenal to surrender the same to the State authorities.

"Resolved further, That in our opinion the governor, as the executive head of the State, may rely upon the sympathy and co-operation of all good citizens in what he may do by authority of the State and her organized military power.

"The foregoing resolutions were, this 6th day of February, 1861, unanimously adopted by a mass meeting of the citizens of Little Rock, Arkansas.

"RICH'D H. JOHNSON,

"Chairman.

"JOHN D. KIMBELL, Secretary."

LITTLE ROCK, ARK., February 12, 1861.

SIR: I have the honor herewith to inclose for the information of the President the originals of four papers relative to my withdrawal from Little Rock Arsenal with my command of the 8th instant.

I forwarded by mail copies of these papers on the 9th of this month, and now inclose the originals by General S.H. Hempstead, of Little Rock, a reliable gentleman, who has politely offered to deliver to you any communication I may wish to send.

For any additional information concerning my retiring from Little Rock I have the honor to refer you to my letters of previous dates. I shall also be most happy to explain any point relative to the matter which may not appear clear already from my past communications.

I beg also to refer to Adjutant-General to the bearer of this, General Hempstead, for much information which it did not appear to me necessary to make known officially. I refer more particularly here to the rumored action taken by the governor of Arkansas to collect forces at Little Rock for the purpose of seizing the arsenal, and also to the views of his conduct and that of his friends and counsellors, taken by the city of Little Rock in its public meetings and the meetings of its council very recently.

I inclose a copy of my letter of transmittal of the 9th instant (inclosed then), with the copies of the original papers now forwarded. [Inclosure E.]

Very respectfully, your obedient servant,

JAS. TOTTEN,

Captain, Second Artillery.

ADJUTANT-GENERAL U. S. ARMY.

[Inclosure B.]

LITTLE ROCK ARSENAL,

Little Rock, Ark., February 6, 1861.

SIR: In the present trying circumstances by which the undersigned finds himself surrounded, as a Federal officer, he is anxious to learn officially from your excellency, before answering your demands for the surrender of the U.S. Arsenal at this place, the following important points, viz:

1st. If this arsenal and all the munitions of war stored therein are left instant as at the hour of 3 o'clock p. m. to-morrow, by the United States forces now in charge of them, will the governor of the States of Arkansas officially take charge of said arsenal and munitions of war in the name of the United States Government, and hold them in that light until future circumstances shall legally absolve him for the responsibility?

2nd. If the United States forces now garrisoning Little Rock Arsenal evacuate said post, and leave the monitions of war intact as at the hour of 3 o'clock p.m. to-morrow, will the governor o the State of Arkansas officially guarantee to said forces an unmolested passage through the State in any direction the officer commanding said troops may elect, and guarantee, moreover, to said forces that right of carrying with them all the public and private property they brought with them to said arsenal, all which has been purchased for or by them, and all which has been sent to them since stationed at said arsenal, consisting of ordnance and ordnance stores, clothing, camp and garrison equipage, and barracks and mess furniture, as also provisions and all their individual or private property.

3rd. If the arsenal and monitions of war stored therein are left intact as at the hour of 3 o'clock p.m. to-morrow, will the governor of Arkansas, in his official capacity, guarantee to the United States forces now in charge therefor the right of marching away from said place with all the honor due to them as Federal officers and soldiers who do not surrender their trust, but simply evacuate a post for want of instructions from their superiors in office, and in doubt as to the propriety of bringing on civil war among their fellow-countrymen?

Explicit and entailed answers to each and every one of these questions will have great influence upon the undersigned in his answer to the communication of the governor of Arkansas, which is promised by 3 o'clock p.m. to-morrow.

I am, very respectfully,

JAMES TOTTEN,

Captain, Second Artillery, Commanding Post.

His Excellency HENRY M. RECTOR, Governor of Arkansas.

EXECUTIVE OFFICE,

Little Rock, Ark., February 7, 1861.

Captain JAMES TOTTEN, U.S. Army,

In charge of U.S. Arsenal, Little Rock:

SIR: Your communication of the 6th instant (yesterday), propounding to myself certain propositions, explicit and detailed answers to which would have great influence upon you in your answer promised the governor of Arkansas by 3 p.m. to-day, was received at about 11 o'clock this morning.

After mature reflection I propose to accept yours first, second, and third propositions, with the following understanding: That being informed your command brought no cannon with you-so none are to be taken away. You shall have a safe passage out of the State in any direction you may please with your command, provided, however, you do not station yourself within the limits of the State of Arkansas or on the borders thereof.

Whatever your command, either of private or public property, brought with them you will be permitted to take away.

I have the honor to be, captain, respectfully, your obedient servant,
HENRY M. RECTOR,
Governor of Arkansas.

[Inclosure D.]
LITTLE ROCK, ARK., February 8, 1861.
Memorandum this day made and signed by James Totten, captain of Second Artillery, in the Army of the United States, and Henry M. Rector, governor of the State of Arkansas.

This paper, marked A,* signed by us, is the demand made by the governor upon Captain Totten for the deliver of the U.S. Arsenal at this place to the State authorities. the paper marked B, signed by us, is a copy of the response of Captain Totten to that communication. The paper marked C, signed by us, is the response of the governor accepting, as therein stated, the terms of the paper B.

It is further witnessed, that on this day, at the hour of 12 m., said Captain Totten, with his command, doth retire from said arsenal, and delivered the same, with all its stores, arms, and monitions of war, intact, to the governor of Arkansas, pursuant to the tenor and purport of said papers A, B, C. And the said Captain James Totten protests that he had thus acted because in the presence of a greatly superior armed force, and which he became satisfied would soon become overwhelming by re-enforcements in case of resistance, involving the sacrifice of his command, without regard to the probable loss of life on the part of the assailants; because any defense of the arsenal in the city of Little Rock, whether successful or unsuccessful, would necessarily involve, to a greater or less extent, the destruction of property in the city, and the loss of lives of the peaceful citizens and families dwelling therein; because, being without instructions from his Government, he took, of necessity, the responsibility of doing what he thought proper and best under all the circumstances, desiring to avoid cause of civil war in this Government, by the first instance of a hostile and bloody collision, yet protesting for himself and in the name of his Government against events beyond his control, and which have actuated him to this course.

(Signed in duplicate.)
HENRY M. RECTOR,
Governor of Arkansas.
JAS. TOTTEN,
Captain, Second Artillery, Commanding Little Rock arsenal.

[Inclosure E.]
LITTLE ROCK, ARK., February 9, 1861.
SIR: I have the honor herewith to inclose for the information of the President copies of four distinct papers relative to a solemn and ever-to-be-regretted act which had been force upon me through the necessities of the circumstances surrounding me. The papers marked A, B, C, and D explain the whole sad affair from beginning to end, in connection with information previously communicated, and comment on my part, therefore, seems unnecessary at present. I have been forced, as the inclosed papers will show, to retire with my command from Little Rock Arsenal, and yield my charge into the hands of Henry M. Rector, governor of the State of Arkansas, who has taken charge of the same in the name of the United States, to hold it in that light until legally absolved from the trust.

I hope I have acted in the whole matter in a manner which will meet the approbation of the Federal authorities. My object throughout these trying circumstances has been to avoid bringing about bloodshed and civil war in this immediate vicinity among peaceable, law-abiding, and loyal citizens of the United States. In doing so, I sincerely believe, in the absence of all instructions, I have only done what appears to be the course indicated by the present administration in this past course, so far as I am informed. It gratifies me beyond measure to be able, on this occasion, to bear honest testimony to the honorable, high-toned, loyal, and law-abiding action taken by the great majority of the most respectable citizen of Little Rock. From the richest to the poorest, I am happy to say, there was but one sentiment, and that was in opposition to the course of the governor and those who counseled and aided him in the deed done.

I am, very respectfully, your obedient servant,
JAS. TOTTEN,
Captain, Second Artillery, Commanding.
Colonel S. COOPER,
Adjutant-General U. S. Army, Washington City, D.C.

[Inclosure F.]
ORDERS, HEADQUARTERS LITTLE ROCK ARSENAL,
Numbers 3.

Little Rock, Ark., February 8, 1861.

The troops of this command, consisting of Company F, Second Artillery, and all the enlisted men of the Ordnance Department, will be prepared to move to-day from this post to a camp to be selected by the commanding officer on the banks of the Arkansas River.

The command will depart as soon as the necessary transportation can be provided.

By order of Captain Totten:

ST. CLAIR DEARING,

Second Lieutenant, Second Artillery, Post Adjutant.

LITTLE ROCK, ARK., February 10, 1861.

SIR: In answer to your telegram dated Washington, February 9, 1861, I this morning answered by telegraph as follows:

I have retired with my command from Little Rock Arsenal, and the governor of Arkansas, in the name of the United States, has charge of all the public property, to hold the same until legally absolved from the trust. I have reported particulars by mail, and shall duplicate them, and explain the whole matter thoroughly. I shall order and proceed with my command to Saint Louis, where I beg that orders may be sent me for my future guidance.

I am, very respectfully, your obedient servant,

JAS. TOTTEN,

Captain, Second Artillery.

Colonel S. COOPER,

Adjutant-General U. S. Army, Washington City, D.C.

ORDERS, CAMP AT FLETCHER'S LANDING,

Numbers 6.

Vicinity of Little Rock, Ark., February 12, 1861.

This command, consisting of Company F, Second Artillery, and the enlisted men of the Ordnance Department formerly garrisoning Little Rock Arsenal, will embark to-day on the steamboat *Madora*, and proceed direct to Saint Louis, Mo., and reported to the general commanding the Department of the West for orders as to its future movements.

JAMES TOTTEN,

Captain, Second Artillery, Commanding.

U.S. SENATE, Washington, February 7, 1861.

His Excellency H.M. RECTOR, Little Rock, Ark.:

The motives which impelled capture of forts other States do not exist in ours. It is all premature. We implore you prevent attack on arsenal if Totten resists.

R.W. JOHNSON.

W.K. SEBASTIAN.

WASHINGTON, February 7, 1861.

R.H. JOHNSON, JAMES B. JOHNSON, Little Rock:

Southern States which captured first were in the act of seceding, were threatened with troops, and their ports and commerce endangered. Not so with us. If Totten resists, for God's sake deliberate and go stop the assault.

R.W. JOHNSON.

WASHINGTON, February 7, 1861.

JOHN POPE, Esq., Little Rock, Ark.:

For God's sake to do not complicate matters by an attack. It will be premature and do incalculable injury. We cannot justify it. The reasons that existed elsewhere for seizure do not exist with us.

ALBERT PIKE.

R.W. JOHNSON.

Appendix C

Reports of the Capture of Fort Smith

FORT SMITH, ARK., April 24, 1861.
COLONEL: I have the honor to report that a body of troops of the State of Arkansas, under the command of Colonel S. Borland, entered and of the First Cavalry, having evacuated it but a few hours previous. Being on a visit at the post at the time, I was made a prisoner of war by the authority of his excellency the governor of the State, but permitted to go at large upon giving my parole not to fight against the State of Arkansas or the Southern Confederated States during the pending difficulties between the latter and the United States, unless exchanged.

In a conversation with Colonel Borland to-day I am given to understand that the governor is acting as though the State had already seceded; that last act in the drama being only a question of a few days' time.

Very respectfully, your obedient servant,
W.C. GATLIN,
Major, Fifth Infantry.

CAMP ON WALNUT CREEK, KANS., May 21, 1861.
SIR: I avail myself of the first opportunity which has occurred since leaving Fort Smith, Ark., to inform you that I evacuated that post at 9 o'clock p. m on the 23rd ultimo, and marched with my command for Fort Washita, where we arrived on the 30th ultimo, and reported for duty to Colonel W.H. Emory, First Cavalry. All the available transportation at the post, amounting to some twenty wagons and teams, was taken along. The ordnance sergeant, hospital steward, chief bugler, sick, and laundresses were left at the post, to be shipped to Jefferson Barracks by Captain A. Montgomery, A.Q.M.

The causes which induce me to evacuate the post I presume are known to the department commander from general notoriety. After the supplies were cut off by the State of Arkansas the post, of course, became untenable, and we could have occupied it in any case but a few more days. One hour after we left, two boats arrived with three hundred men and ten pieces of artillery. To have contended against this force with two companies of cavalry, and that, too, while the entire population of the surrounding country were ready at a moment's warning to take up arms against us, could only have resulted eventually in our being taken prisoners and the loss to the Government of all the arms, horses, means of transportation, &c., at the post.

I have the honor to be, sir, very respectfully, your obedient servant,

S.D. STURGIS,

Captain, First Cavalry.

FORT SMITH, ARK., April 24, 1861.

CAPTAIN: I have the honor to report that the companies of cavalry under command of Captain Sturgis, First Cavalry, withdrew from this post yesterday evening and marched in the direction of Fort Washita. I inclose a copy of an order he issued immediately before leaving, directing the entire evacuation of the post.

About two hours after his departure a body of troops under the command of Colonel Solon Borland, aide-de-camp to his excellency the governor of the State of Arkansas, accompanied by the adjutant-general of the State, arrived in steamers and took possession of the post, making me a prisoner of war, under authority and by direction of the governor of the State. Major R.C. Gatlin, Fifth Infantry, who happened to be in the garrison at the time on visit, was also made prisoner of war. On giving our parole that we would not fight against the State of Arkansas or the Southern Confederate States during the existing difficulties between the latter and the United States, unless exchanged, we were permitted to go at large. The force under Colonel Borland consisted of 235 men, rank and file, with battery of artillery. Colonel Borland demanded and has taken possession of all the public property at the post and in this vicinity, inventories of all the public property at the post and in its vicinity, inventories of which will be forwarded to the proper bureau.

For the information of the friends of the parties. I beg leave to state that Major Brown, paymaster, and Captain Burns, C.S., were absent from the post at the time of its evacuation. Major Brown, returning from Fort Arbuckle, received information at Scullyvile that I had been made a prisoner of war, and immediately turned back and joined Captain Sturgis' command. Captain Burns had gone down the river to look after certain subsistence stores, which it was feared would be seized by the State authorities.

The movement of Captain Sturgis was necessitated by the limited supply of provisions on hand and the intelligence received a short time before he left that all the public stores on the river in transit to this post had been detained or captured by the State authorities. He was also awarded that the governor of the State had dispatched a force, with artillery, to demand possession of the post, and possibly to capture his arms and horses. It was not expected that any orders had been given to make prisoners of war.

I have the honor to be, sir, very respectfully, your obedient servant,

A. MONTGOMERY,

Captain and Qu. M., U.S. Army.

Appendix D

Items Held by the Little Rock Arsenal on February 9, 1861

Weapons

M1822 .69 caliber (flintlock)	5,625
M1822 .69 caliber (percussion-converted)	53
M1842. 69 caliber smoothbore (percussion)	357
M1855 .58 caliber rifle musket	900
M1817 common rifle	125
M1841 rifle	54
M1847 musketoon	2
Hall's carbine	267
Hall's rifle (flintlock)	2,864
TOTAL	10,247

Other Items

250,000 musket cartridges
520,000 percussion caps
4 bronze cannons

Notes

Introduction

1. James Woods, *Rebellion and Realignment: Arkansas's Road to Secession* (Fayetteville: University of Arkansas Press, 1987), 177.
2. Ibid., 171; William O'Donnell, *The Civil War Quadrennium: A Narrative History of Day-to-Day Life in Little Rock, Arkansas During the American War Between the States, 1861-1865* (Little Rock: Civil War Roundtable of Arkansas, 1985), III.
3. John Harrell, *Confederate Military History*, Volume X (New York: Thomas Yoseloff, 1962).
4. David Thomas, *Arkansas in War and Reconstruction: 1861–1874* (Little Rock: Arkansas Division, United Daughters of the Confederacy, 1926).
5. Michael Dougan, *Confederate Arkansas: The People and Policies of a Frontier State in Wartime* (Tuscaloosa: University of Alabama Press, 1976).

Chapter 1

6. Brian Walton, "How Many Voted in Arkansas Elections Before the Civil War?" *Arkansas Historical Quarterly* 39 (Spring 1980): 70; Thomas DeBlack, *With Fire and Sword: Arkansas, 1861–1874* (Fayetteville: University of Arkansas, 2003), 17-18.

7. *Arkansas Gazette*, October 13, 1860.
8. Little Rock, *Arkansian*, November 24, 1861; Thomas DeBlack, "Prosperity and Peril: Arkansas in the Late Antebellum Period," in *Arkansas: A Narrative History*, Jeannie Whayne, et al. (Fayetteville: University of Arkansas Press, 2002) 160–61.
9. Inaugural address of Governor Henry M. Rector, *Arkansas Gazette*, November 24, 1860.
10. Waddy W. Moore, "Henry Massie Rector," in *The Governors of Arkansas: Essays in Political Biography*, eds. Timothy Donovan and Willard Gatewood (Fayetteville: University of Arkansas Press, 1981), 30–31; Dougan, "A Look at the 'Family' in Arkansas Politics, 1858–1865," 102.
11. *Little Rock Old Line Democrat*, May 24, 1860; Jeannie Whayne, Michael Dougan, and Waddy Moore, s.v. "Henry Massie Rector," *The Encyclopedia of Arkansas History & Culture*, http://www.encyclopediaofarkansas.net/encyclopedia/entry-detail.aspx?entryID=119 (accessed January 3, 2013); Thomas DeBlack, "The Family [Political Dynasty]," *The Encyclopedia of Arkansas History & Culture*, http://www.encyclopediaofarkansas.net/encyclopedia/entry-detail.aspx?search=1&entryID=2666 (accessed January 3, 2013).
12. Dougan, *Confederate Arkansas*, 36–38; Orville Taylor, *Negro Slavery in Arkansas* (Fayetteville: University of Arkansas Press, 2000), 52.
13. Dougan, *Confederate Arkansas*, 36–38.
14. Woods, *Rebellion and Realignment*, 119–20; Dougan, *Confederate Arkansas*, 37–38.
15. Dougan, *Confederate Arkansas*, 39–40; Woods, *Rebellion and Realignment*, 74–75; *Arkansas Gazette*, December 15, 1860.
16. Ralph Wooster, "The Arkansas Secession Convention," *Arkansas Historical Quarterly* 13 (Summer 1954): 173.
17. Jack Scoggs, "Arkansas in the Secession Crisis," *Arkansas Historical Quarterly* 12 (Autumn 1953): 195-196.

Chapter 2

18. James Eison, "The Arsenal in Little Rock," *Pulaski County Historical Review* 16 (June 1968): 17.
19. Duane Huddleston, "Building the Little Rock Arsenal," *Pulaski County Historical Review* 20 (December 1972): 45.
20. Eison, "The Arsenal in Little Rock," 17. Some sources name Lieutenant F.L. James as the officer tasked with the purchase of the property.

21. Huddleston, "Building the Little Rock Arsenal," 45.
22. *Arkansas Gazette*, May 30, 1837; Huddleston, "Building the Little Rock Arsenal," 45.
23. Huddleston, "Building the Little Rock Arsenal," 45.
24. *Arkansas Gazette*, June 27, 1838; Huddleston, "Building the Little Rock Arsenal," 46.
25. *Arkansas Gazette*, June 27, 1838; Huddleston, "Building the Little Rock Arsenal," 46.
26. Philip Van Doren Stern, *Soldier Life in the Union and Confederate Armies* (Bonanza Books: New York, 1961), 159–60; Thomas Ezell, "'To Avoid an Effusion of Blood…': The Little Rock Crisis of 1861" (Unpublished paper, n.d.); *Arkansas Gazette*, March 3, 1841. Sutlers were private merchants who were allowed by local commanding officers to set up shop near army posts. These businesses provided soldiers with food that was not typically found in their daily rations and also sold personal items such as writing utensils.
27. Edwin Bearss and Arrell Gibson, *Fort Smith: Little Gibraltar on the Arkansas* (Norman: University of Oklahoma Press, 1979), 19–21, 90, 113, 136; Edwin Bearss, "In Quest of Peace on the Indian Border: The Establishment of Fort Smith," *Arkansas Historical Quarterly* 23 (Summer 1964): 139–44; James Haskett, "The Final Chapter in the Story of the First Fort Smith," *Arkansas Historical Quarterly* 25 (Autumn 1966): 219, 220, 228; Ruth Mapes, *Old Fort Smith: Cultural Center on the Southwestern Frontier* (Little Rock: Pioneer Press, 1965), 6–7.
28. Richard Trotter, "For the Defense of the Western Border: Arkansas Volunteers on the Indian Frontier, 1846–1847," *Arkansas Historical Quarterly* 60 (Winter 2001): 394; Bearss and Gibson, *Fort Smith*, 239.
29. Ezell, "Little Rock Crisis of 1861"; Report of Colonel Samuel Cooper, Adjutant General of the United States Army, January 18, 1861. *The War of the Rebellion: A Compilation of the Official Records of the Union and Confederate Armies* (Washington: 1880–1901), Series III, Volume I, pp. 47–48. (Hereby cited afterward as *O.R.*)
30. Report of Colonel Henry Craig, Chief of Ordnance, November 12, 1859, *O.R.*, Series III, Volume I, 1; Report of Colonel Henry Craig, January 15, 1861, *O.R.*, Series III, Volume I, 39; Report of Colonel Henry Craig, January 21, 1861, *O.R.*, Series III, Volume I, 42–23.
31. Report of Colonel Henry Craig, January 21, 1861, *O.R.*, Series III, Volume I, 42–23; Ezell, "Little Rock Crisis of 1861."
32. David Sesser, "James Totten," *The Encyclopedia of Arkansas History & Culture*, http://www.encyclopediaofarkansas.net/encyclopedia/entry-detail.aspx?search=1&entryID=4452 (accessed January 3, 2013).
33. Ezell, "Little Rock Crisis of 1861."

CHAPTER 3

34. Ezell, "Little Rock Crisis of 1861."
35. Governor Henry Rector, Correspondence with Captain James Totten, January 29, 1861, *O.R.*, Series I, Volume I, 638–39.
36. Captain James Totten, Correspondence with Governor Henry Rector, January 29, 1861, *O.R.*, Series I, Volume I, 639.
37. Ezell, "Little Rock Crisis of 1861."
38. O'Donnell, *The Civil War Quadrennium*, 5–6.
39. Captain James Totten, Correspondence with Colonel Samuel Cooper, January 29, 1861, *O.R.*, Series I, Volume I, 638.
40. Philip Shriver Klein, *President James Buchanan: A Biography* (University Park: Pennsylvania State University Press, 1962), 160; Jean Baker, *James Buchanan* (New York: Times Books, 2004), 72-73.
41. Elbert Smith, *The Presidency of James Buchanan* (Lawrence: University Press of Kansas, 1975), 27–28, 39–46, 81; Klein, *President James Buchanan*, 314–15.
42. Bruce Allardice, *Confederate Colonels: A Biographical Register* (Columbia: University of Missouri Press, 2008), 183; Margret Ross, *Arkansas Gazette: The Early Years, 1819–1866* (Little Rock: Arkansas Gazette Foundation, 1969), 352; Harrell, *Confederate Military History*, 6–7.
43. Harrell, *Confederate Military History*, 7.
44. *Journal of Both Sessions of the Convention of the State of Arkansas* (Little Rock: Johnson and Yerkes, State Printer, 1861), 48; Dougan, *Confederate Arkansas*, 41; Ross, *Arkansas Gazette*, 352.
45. Ross, *Arkansas Gazette*, 352–53; Harrell, *Confederate Military History*, 8.
46. Harrell, *Confederate Military History*, 8; Mauriel Joslyn, "Patrick Ronayne Cleburne (1828–1864)," *The Encyclopedia of Arkansas History & Culture*, http://www.encyclopediaofarkansas.net/encyclopedia/entry-detail.aspx?search=1&entryID=339 (accessed January 3, 2013).
47. Thomas Robson Hay, *Cleburne and His Command* (Wilmington, N.C.; Broadfoot Publishing, 1991), 74–75, 76–77, 78; Howell and Elizabeth Purdue, *Pat Cleburne: Confederate General* (Hillsboro, Texas; Hill Junior College Press, 1973), 44–45, 46–49, 50–52; Joslyn, "Patrick Ronayne Cleburne."
48. Craig Symonds, *Stonewall of the West: Patrick Cleburne and the Civil War* (Lawrence: University Press of Kansas, 1997), 47; Purdue and Purdue, *Pat Cleburne*, 63–64; Hay, *Cleburne and His Command*, 79, 82.
49. Purdue and Purdue, *Pat Cleburne*, 70; Symonds, *Stonewall of the West*, 46; Scoggs, "Arkansas in the Secession Crisis," 201; Ezell, "Little Rock Crisis of 1861."

50. Ross, *Arkansas Gazette*, 353; *Journal of Both Sessions*, 48–49.
51. Mary Lysobey, "Montgomery County," *The Encyclopedia of Arkansas History & Culture*, http://www.encyclopediaofarkansas.net/encyclopedia/entry-detail.aspx?search=1&entryID=793 (accessed January 3, 2013).
52. Resolution of the Little Rock City Council, February 5, 1861, *O.R.*, Series I, Volume I, 641.
53. Ibid., February 6, 1861, 641–42.
54. Ibid., 642.

Chapter 4

55. Walter Brown, *A Life of Albert Pike* (Fayetteville: University of Arkansas Press, 1997), 227–28.
56. Walter Brown, "The Mexican War Experiences of Albert Pike and the 'Mounted Devils' of Arkansas, *Arkansas Historical Quarterly* XII (Winter 1953), 301–2; Brown, *Life of Albert Pike*, 228, 229.
57. Brown, *Life of Albert Pike*, 230, 231; William Frazier, "Rackensack in the Field: Arkansans in the U.S.-Mexican War," in *Ready, Booted, and Spurred: Arkansas in the U.S. Mexican War*, ed. Mark Christ (Little Rock: Butler Center Books, 2009), 43.
58. Frazier, "Rackensack in the Field," 48–49.
59. Ibid., 54, 64.
60. Brown, *Life of Albert Pike*, 236–39.
61. Ibid., 240.
62. Ezell, "Little Rock Crisis of 1861."
63. O'Donnell, *Civil War Quadrennium*, III–V; Billy Higgins, "Act 151 of 1859," *Encyclopedia of Arkansas History and Culture*, http://www.encyclopediaofarkansas.net/encyclopedia/entry-detail.aspx?entryID=4430, accessed July 7, 2013.
64. Ezell, "Little Rock Crisis of 1861."
65. Ibid.
66. M.V. Bowks de la Rosa, "Pike-Roane Duel," *The Encyclopedia of Arkansas History & Culture*, http://www.encyclopediaofarkansas.net/encyclopedia/entry-detail.aspx?search=1&entryID=4536 (accessed July 10, 2013); Ezell, "Little Rock Crisis of 1861."
67. Bobby Roberts, "John Selden Roane," in *Arkansas Biography: A Collection of Notable Lives*, ed. Nancy Williams (Fayetteville: University of Arkansas Press, 2000), 241–42.

68. Captain James Totten, Correspondence with Colonel Samuel Cooper, February 6, 1861, *O.R.*, Series I, Volume I, 639.
69. Ezell, "Little Rock Crisis of 1861."
70. Governor Henry Rector, Correspondence with Captain James Totten, February 6, 1861, *O.R.*, Series I, Volume I, 640.
71. Ibid.
72. Ezell, "Little Rock Crisis of 1861."
73. Captain James Totten, Correspondence with Governor Henry Rector, February 6, 1861, *O.R.*, Series I, Volume I, 643.
74. Robert Ward Johnson and William King Sebastian to Henry Rector, February 7, 1861. *O.R.*, Series I, Volume I, 681.
75. Robert Ward Johnson to R.H. Johnson and James B. Johnson, February 7, 1861. *O.R.*, Series I, Volume I, 681–82.
76. Albert Pike and Robert Ward Johnson to John Pope, February 7, 1861. *O.R.*, Series I, Volume I, 682.
77. Robert Ward Johnson and Thomas C. Hindman to Henry Rector, February 7, 1861. *O.R.*, Series I, Volume I, 683.
78. Henry Rector to James Totten, February 7, 1861, *O.R.*, Series I, Volume I, 644.
79. Memorandum by Henry Rector and James Totten, February 8, 1861, *O.R.*, Series I, Volume I, 644–45; Orders Number 3, St. Clair Dearing, February 8, 1861, *O.R.*, Series I, Volume I, 645.
80. Ezell, "Little Rock Crisis of 1861"; Memorandum by Henry Rector and James Totten, February 8, 1861, *O.R.*, Series I, Volume I, 644–45.
81. Ezell, "Little Rock Crisis of 1861."
82. James Totten to Samuel Cooper, February 9, 1861, *O.R.*, Series I, Volume I, 645; James Totten to Samuel Cooper, February 10, 1861, *O.R.*, Series I, Volume I, 646.
83. Ezell, "Little Rock Crisis of 1861."
84. Orders Number 6, James Totten, February 12, 1861, *O.R.*, Series I, Volume I, 646.

Chapter 5

85. Woods, *Rebellion and Realignment*, 130.
86. Wooster, "The Arkansas Secession Convention," 180, 182–83.
87. Report of Major Justus McKinstry, February 12, 1861, *O.R.*, Series I, Volume I, 646–47.

88. David Sesser, "A Confederate Arkansan: The Civil War Career of Major General Thomas James Churchill" (master's thesis, Henderson State University, 2011), 17; Report of Captain William Burns, April 19, 1861, *O.R.*, Series I, Volume I, 647.
89. Edmund Burgevin to Colonel Lorenzo Thomas, April 27, 1861, *O.R.*, Series I, Volume I, 674; Henry Rector to Simon Cameron, April 22, 1861, *O.R.*, Series I, Volume I, 687.
90. Report of Captain William Burns, April 21, 1861, *O.R.*, Series I, Volume I, 647.
91. E.D. Townsend to Lieutenant Colonel William Emory, April 17, 1861. *O.R.*, Series I, Volume I, 667.
92. Report of Major Samuel Sturgis, May 21, 1861, *O.R.*, Series I, Volume I, 650–51; Report of Captain Alexander Montgomery, April 24, 1861, *O.R.*, Series I, Volume I, 650; Bearss and Gibson, *Fort Smith*, 242. It is unclear exactly how much time passed between Sturgis's departure and the arrival of the Arkansas troops under the command of Borland. Sturgis reported that it was just one hour while Montgomery reported that it was at least two hours.
93. Report of Brigadier General B. Burroughs, May 8, 1861, *O.R.*, Series I, Volume I, 691.
94. Wooster, "Arkansas Secession Convention," 184.

CONCLUSION

95. Moore, "Henry Massie Rector," 32; Michael Dougan, "Harris Flanagin," in *The Governors of Arkansas: Essays in Political Biography*, eds. Timothy Donovan and Willard Gatewood (Fayetteville: University of Arkansas Press, 1981), 34.
96. Sesser, "James Totten."
97. Joslyn, "Patrick Ronayne Cleburne."
98. Carl Moneyhon, "Thomas Carmichael Hindman," in *Arkansas Biography: A Collection of Notable Lives*, ed. Nancy Smith (Fayetteville: University of Arkansas Press, 2000), 142–43; Diane Neal and Thomas Kremm, *The Lion of the South: General Thomas C. Hindman* (Macon, GA: Mercer University Press, 1993), 108, 175, 233.
99. Brown, *Life of Albert Pike*, 321, 353, 426; Carl Moneyhon, "Albert Pike," in *Arkansas Biography: A Collection of Notable Lives*, ed. Nancy Smith (Fayetteville: University of Arkansas Press, 2000), 223–24; Fred Allsopp, *Albert Pike: A Biography* (Kila, MT: Kessinger, 1992), 193–94.

100. Michael Dougan, "David Walker," *Encyclopedia of Arkansas History and Culture*, http://www.encyclopediaofarkansas.net/encyclopedia/entry-detail.aspx?search=1&entryID=3237 (accessed July 29, 2013).
101. William Shea, "Isaac Murphy," in *Arkansas Biography: A Collection of Notable Lives*, ed. Nancy Smith (Fayetteville: University of Arkansas Press, 2000), 206–7.
102. Bobby Roberts, "John Selden Roane," in *Arkansas Biography: A Collection of Notable Lives*, ed. Nancy Smith (Fayetteville: University of Arkansas Press, 2000), 241–42.
103. James Woods, "Solon Borland," in *Arkansas Biography: A Collection of Notable Lives*, ed. Nancy Smith (Fayetteville: University of Arkansas Press, 2000), 32–33.
104. Ezra Warner, *Generals in Blue: Lives of the Union Commanders* (Baton Rouge: Louisiana State University Press, 2006), 486-487.
105. Dallas Herndon, *Centennial History of Arkansas* (Easley, SC: Southern Historical Press, 1922), Vol. 1, 327.
106. Bearss and Gibson, *Fort Smith*, 242–45; David Bowden, "United States District Court for the Western District of Arkansas, *Encyclopedia of Arkansas History & Culture*, http://www.encyclopediaofarkansas.net/encyclopedia/entry-detail.aspx?entryID=1162 (accessed July 29, 2013); Jeremy Lynch, "Fort Smith National Historic Site," *Encyclopedia of Arkansas History & Culture*, http://www.encyclopediaofarkansas.net/encyclopedia/entry-detail.aspx?search=1&entryID=4522 (accessed July 29, 2013).
107. Ezell, "The Little Rock Crisis of 1861."
108. Michael Banasik, ed., *Confederate "Tales of the War" in the Trans-Mississippi, Part One: 1861* (Iowa City: Camp Pope Bookshop, 2010), 53–54, 74.
109. Lawrence Sanders, "David Owen Dodd," in *Arkansas Biography: A Collection of Notable Lives*, ed. Nancy Smith (Fayetteville: University of Arkansas Press, 2000), 84–85.
110. John Spurgeon, "Douglass MacArthur," *Encyclopedia of Arkansas History & Culture*, http://www.encyclopediaofarkansas.net/encyclopedia/entry-detail.aspx?search=1&entryID=2768 (accessed July 30, 2013).
111. Eison, "Arsenal in Little Rock," 21; Logan, "Something So Dim," 20; MacArthur Museum of Arkansas Military History, "Tower Building of the Little Rock Arsenal Timeline," accessed July 30, 2013, http://www.arkmilitaryheritage.com/about/timeln.htm; Arkansas Arts Center, "History + Mission," accessed July 20, 2013, http://www.arkarts.com/page.aspx?pid=564.

Bibliography

Allardice, Bruce. *Confederate Colonels: A Biographical Register*. Columbia: University of Missouri Press, 2008.

Allsopp, Fred. *Albert Pike: A Biography*. Kila, MT: Kessinger, 1992.

Baker, Jean. *James Buchanan*. New York: Times Books, 2004.

Banasik, Michael, ed. *Confederate "Tales of the War" in the Trans-Mississippi, Part One: 1861*. Iowa City, IA: Camp Pope Bookshop, 2010.

Bearss, Edwin. "In Quest of Peace on the Indian Border: The Establishment of Fort Smith," *Arkansas Historical Quarterly* 23 (Summer 1964).

Bearss, Edwin, and Arrell Gibson. *Fort Smith: Little Gibraltar on the Arkansas*. Norman: University of Oklahoma Press, 1979.

Bowden, David. "United States District Court for the Western District of Arkansas, Encyclopedia of Arkansas History & Culture." http://www.encyclopediaofarkansas.net/encyclopedia/entry-detail.aspx?entryID=1162.

Bowks de la Rosa, M.V. "Pike-Roane Duel." *The Encyclopedia of Arkansas History & Culture*, http://www.encyclopediaofarkansas.net/encyclopedia/entry-detail.aspx?search=1&entryID=4536.

Brown, Walter. *A Life of Albert Pike*. Fayetteville: University of Arkansas Press, 1997.

———. "The Mexican War Experiences of Albert Pike and the 'Mounted Devils' of Arkansas." *Arkansas Historical Quarterly* XII (Winter 1953).

DeBlack, Thomas. "The Family [Political Dynasty]," *The Encyclopedia of Arkansas History & Culture*, http://www.encyclopediaofarkansas.net/encyclopedia/entry-detail.aspx?search=1&entryID=2666.

———. *With Fire and Sword: Arkansas, 1861–1874*. Fayetteville: University of Arkansas, 2003.

Donovan, Timothy, and Willard Gatewood, eds. *The Governors of Arkansas: Essays in Political Biography*. Fayetteville: University of Arkansas Press, 1981.

Dougan, Michael. *Confederate Arkansas: The People and Policies of a Frontier State in Wartime*. Tuscaloosa: University of Alabama Press, 1976.

———. "David Walker," *Encyclopedia of Arkansas History and Culture*, http://www.encyclopediaofarkansas.net/encyclopedia/entry-detail.aspx?search=1&entryID=3237.

———. "A Look at the 'Family' in Arkansas Politics, 1858–1865." *Arkansas Historical Quarterly* 29 (Summer 1970).

Eison, James. "The Arsenal in Little Rock." *Pulaski County Historical Review* 16 (June 1968).

Ezell, Thomas. "'To Avoid an Effusion of Blood…': The Little Rock Crisis of 1861." Unpublished paper, n.d.

Frazier, William. "Rackensack in the Field: Arkansans in the U.S.-Mexican War," in *Ready, Booted, and Spurred: Arkansas in the U.S. Mexican War*, ed. Mark Christ. Little Rock: Butler Center Books, 2009.

Harrell, John M. *Confederate Military History*, Volume X. New York: Thomas Yoseloff, 1962.

Haskett, James. "The Final Chapter in the Story of the First Fort Smith." *Arkansas Historical Quarterly* 25 (Autumn 1966).

Hay, Thomas Robson. *Cleburne and His Command*. Wilmington, NC: Broadfoot Publishing, 1991.

Herndon, Dallas. *Centennial History of Arkansas*. Vol. 1. Easley, SC: Southern Historical Press, 1922.

Higgins, Billy. "Act 151 of 1859," *Encyclopedia of Arkansas History and Culture*, http://www.encyclopediaofarkansas.net/encyclopedia/entry-detail.aspx?entryID=4430.

Huddleston, Duane. "Building the Little Rock Arsenal." *Pulaski County Historical Review* 20 (December 1972).

Joslyn, Mauriel. "Patrick Ronayne Cleburne (1828–1864)," *The Encyclopedia of Arkansas History & Culture*, http://www.encyclopediaofarkansas.net/encyclopedia/entry-detail.aspx?search=1&entryID=339.

Journal of Both Sessions of the Convention of the State of Arkansas. Little Rock: Johnson and Yerkes, State Printer, 1861

Klein, Philip Shriver. *President James Buchanan: A Biography*. University Park: Pennsylvania State University Press, 1962.

Logan, Charles. "Something so Dim it Must be Holy: Civil War Commemorative Sculpture in Arkansas, 1886–1934." Arkansas Historic Preservation Program, Little Rock.

Lynch, Jeremy. "Fort Smith National Historic Site," *The Encyclopedia of Arkansas History & Culture*, http://www.encyclopediaofarkansas.net/encyclopedia/entry-detail.aspx?search=1&entryID=4522.

Lysobey, Mary. "Montgomery County," *The Encyclopedia of Arkansas History & Culture*, http://www.encyclopediaofarkansas.net/encyclopedia/entry-detail.aspx?search=1&entryID=793.

Mapes, Ruth. *Old Fort Smith: Cultural Center on the Southwestern Frontier.* Little Rock, AR: Pioneer Press, 1965.

Neal, Diane, and Thomas Kremm. *The Lion of the South: General Thomas C. Hindman*. Macon, GA: Mercer University Press, 1993.

O'Donnell, William. *The Civil War Quadrennium: A Narrative History of Day-to-Day Life in Little Rock, Arkansas During the American War Between the States, 1861–1865*. Little Rock: Civil War Roundtable of Arkansas, 1985.

Purdue, Howell, and Elizabeth Purdue. *Pat Cleburne: Confederate General.* Hillsboro, TX: Hill Junior College Press, 1973.

Ross, Margret. *Arkansas Gazette: The Early Years, 1819–1866*. Little Rock: Arkansas Gazette Foundation, 1969.

Scoggs, Jack B. "Arkansas in the Secession Crisis." *Arkansas Historical Quarterly* 12 (Autumn 1953).

Sesser, David. "A Confederate Arkansan: The Civil War Career of Major General Thomas James Churchill." Master's thesis, Henderson State University, 2011.

———. "James Totten." *The Encyclopedia of Arkansas History & Culture*, http://www.encyclopediaofarkansas.net/encyclopedia/entry-detail.aspx?search=1&entryID=4452.

Smith, Elbert. *The Presidency of James Buchanan*. Lawrence: University Press of Kansas, 1975.

Spurgeon, John. "Douglass MacArthur," *The Encyclopedia of Arkansas History & Culture*, http://www.encyclopediaofarkansas.net/encyclopedia/entry-detail.aspx?search=1&entryID=2768.

Stern, Philip Van Doren. *Soldier Life in the Union and Confederate Armies*. Bonanza Books: New York, 1961.

Symonds, Craig. *Stonewall of the West: Patrick Cleburne and the Civil War.* Lawrence: University Press of Kansas, 1997.

Taylor, Orville. *Negro Slavery in Arkansas*. Fayetteville: University of Arkansas Press, 2000.

Thomas, David. *Arkansas in War and Reconstruction: 1861-1874*. Little Rock: Arkansas Division, United Daughters of the Confederacy, 1926.

Trotter, Richard. "For the Defense of the Western Border: Arkansas Volunteers on the Indian Frontier, 1846–1847." *Arkansas Historical Quarterly* 60 (Winter 2001).

Walton, Brian. "How Many Voted in Arkansas Elections Before the Civil War?" *Arkansas Historical Quarterly* 39 (Spring 1980).

Warner, Ezra. *Generals in Blue: Lives of the Union Commanders*. Baton Rouge: Louisiana State University Press, 2006.

The War of the Rebellion: A Compilation of the Official Records of the Union and Confederate Armies. Washington, D.C.: Government Printing Office, 1880–1901.

Whayne, Jeannie, et al. *Arkansas: A Narrative History*. Fayetteville: University of Arkansas Press, 2002.

Whayne, Jeannie, Michael Dougan and Waddy Moore. "Henry Massie Rector," *The Encyclopedia of Arkansas History & Culture*, http://www.encyclopediaofarkansas.net/encyclopedia/entry-detail.aspx?entryID=119.

Williams, Nancy, ed. *Arkansas Biography: A Collection of Notable Lives*. Fayetteville: University of Arkansas Press, 2000.

Woods, James. *Rebellion and Realignment: Arkansas's Road to Secession*. Fayetteville: University of Arkansas Press, 1987.

Wooster, Ralph. "The Arkansas Secession Convention." *Arkansas Historical Quarterly* 13 (Summer 1954).

Websites

Arkansas Arts Center. "History + Mission." http://www.arkarts.com/page.aspx?pid=564.

MacArthur Museum of Arkansas Military History. "Tower Building of the Little Rock Arsenal Timeline." http://www.arkmilitaryheritage.com/about/timeln.htm.

Newspapers

Arkansas Gazette.

Arkansian.

Old Line Democrat.

Index

About the Author

David Sesser is an assistant librarian at Huie Library, Henderson State University in Arkadelphia, Arkansas. He holds graduate degrees in history, public history and library and information science. He resides in Arkadelphia with his wife.

Visit us at
www.historypress.net

This title is also available as an e-book